1634
This edition reprinted in 1992 by Tiger Books International PLC, London
© 1986 Coombe Books
Printed and bound in Singapore
All rights reserved
ISBN 1 85501 116 6

Acknowledgement
The publishers would like to thank the staff of
Art for Eating for their assistance.

Text by
Denise Jarrett-Macauley

Introduction
page 6

PUDDINGS & DESSERTS

**TIGER BOOKS INTERNATIONAL
LONDON**

Contents

Introduction

The most important thing about desserts is to make sure that they complement the rest of the meal. This book aims to provide you with a selection ranging from the simplest fruit dishes for summer meals – such as Melons and Mango on Ice – to hot, winter desserts, such as Apricot Pudding.

Chapter headings, with the exception of 'Special Desserts' and 'Quick Desserts', trace the seasons and reflect the availability of fruits throughout the year. Starting with spring, when not many fruits are available fresh, dishes like Savarin Chantilly and Coffee Pecan Pie make use of ingredients that are available all year round, such as tinned fruit and nuts. Meanwhile, Linzertorte could be a chance to use frozen fruit, and Lemon and Orange Chiffon Flan to use traditional winter and spring fare.

Summer is a time for fresh fruit and cool ices. Sorbets and granitas provide a refreshing and colourful method of serving fruits and their juices. These dishes are easy to make in advance and serve as unusual treats; together with a range of ice creams there is something for every taste and occasion.

Autumn heralds an abundance of fruits, such as plums, pears and apples. All these can be bottled and used in dishes like Honey Plum Cobbler, Pear and Nut Crêpes or Apple Dumplings with Walnut Sauce. Many of the dishes in this section are light, but warming. Red Crumble and Cherry Clafoutis are ideal for chillier, autumn days.

The thought of steamed and suet-based puddings is undeniably linked with winter, with Apple Betty filled with spices and Carrot Pudding served with hot custard on the menu. For the Christmas table a selection of puddings and desserts – such as flaming Yuletide Pudding, Snowballs, and a tangy Pacific Pudding served with orange butter – will set off the festive atmosphere.

Special occasions, of course, can arise at any time of the year and a variety of recipes has been included, some of which take time to prepare but produce spectacular results. Exotic fruits with puréed sauces and glamourously displayed, flaming dishes will provide a breathtaking end to any special meal.

As for the chapter on quick desserts, most of the recipes included can be made from ingredients to be found in one's larder or kitchen cupboard. Poor Knights of Windsor and Caramel Oranges are good examples of simple, easy-to-make dishes which can be made in 15 minutes.

Ingredients in the book are measured for 6 people.

Chocolate Lime Flan

PREPARATION TIME: 20 minutes

225g (8oz) digestive biscuits
75g (3oz) plain chocolate
25g (1oz) butter
350g (12oz) white marshmallows
150ml (¼ pint) milk
2 limes
150ml (5 fl oz) double cream
50g (2oz) plain chocolate, grated
The grated rind of 1 lemon
150ml (5 fl oz) double cream,
*   whipped for decoration*

Crush the biscuits. Melt the chocolate and butter together and mix in the biscuits. Lightly grease the sides and base of a 23cm (9 inch) flan dish. Press the biscuit mixture onto the base and sides of the dish. Melt the marshmallows in a basin over hot water and add the milk. Stir in the juice from one lime and grate the rind. Mix in the lemon rind, whip the double cream and fold into the marshmallow mixture. Pour into the crumb base and leave to set. Decorate the flan with the remaining cream, grated chocolate and slices of the second lime.

Cointreau and Mandarin Mousse

PREPARATION TIME: 10 minutes

290g (10½oz) tin of mandarin
*   oranges*
1 tablespoon gelatine
4 tablespoons Cointreau or orange
*   liqueur*
3 egg yolks
2 tablespoons caster sugar

Strain the mandarins, reserving the juice. Sprinkle the gelatine over the juice. Pour two tablespoons of Cointreau over the mandarins and leave them to soak. Add the remaining Cointreau, egg yolks and sugar to the gelatine. Whisk the egg mixture over a bowl of hot water until thick and frothy (with an electric whisk this should take 4 minutes). Pour into individual glass dishes and chill until set. Spoon the soaked mandarins on top. Serve.

Cheese Mousse with Strawberries

PREPARATION TIME: 45 minutes

200g (7oz) cottage cheese
150g (5oz) strawberries
25g (1oz) icing sugar
2 tablespoons Cointreau or orange
*   liqueur*
2 tablespoons lemon juice
2 tablespoons orange juice
1 tablespoon gelatine
150ml (5 fl oz) double cream
6 meringue rosettes

Chocolate Sauce
215g (8oz) plain chocolate
2 tablespoons milk
25g (1oz) butter

Put the cottage cheese into a bowl and add the strawberries, reserving a few strawberries for decoration. Sift the icing sugar over the cheese and sprinkle over the Cointreau. Cover and leave to stand in the fridge for about half an hour. Heat the orange and lemon juice and dissolve the gelatine in it. Whilst the gelatine is still warm, stir in the cheese mixture. Stiffly whip the cream and fold it in. Serve the mousse on the plate and decorate with the reserved strawberries. Serve with some chocolate sauce and meringue rosettes.

Chocolate Sauce
Melt the chololate, milk and butter in a bowl over hot water. Stir rapidly. Serve.

This page: Chocolate Lime Flan.

Facing page: Cointreau and Mandarin Mousse (top) and Cheese Mousse with Strawberries (bottom).

Spring Desserts

Individual Banana Tarts

PREPARATION TIME: 30 minutes

COOKING TIME: 15 minutes

OVEN: 200°C (400°F) Gas Mark 6

Pastry
75g (3oz) butter
175g (6oz) plain flour
2 tablespoons caster sugar
1 egg yolk
1 tablespoon water

Filling
2 firm bananas
1 teaspoon lemon juice
150ml (5 fl oz) double cream
6oz apricot jam to glaze

Pastry
Place the butter and flour into a bowl and rub to form a breadcrumb-like mixture. Stir in the sugar. Beat together the egg yolk and water and add to flour to form a stiff dough. Lightly knead and chill for ½ hour. Roll out pastry and using a 7.5cm (3 inch) fluted cutter. Press into tartlet tins and bake until golden brown.

Filling
Slice the bananas and sprinkle with the lemon juice. Whisk the cream and fill the pastry cases. Lay the sliced banana in a circle to cover the cream. Melt the apricot jam in a small saucepan and pour over tartlet pastry cases, making sure all the bananas are glazed. Serve cold.

Coffee Pecan Pie

PREPARATION TIME: 20 minutes
plus chilling

175g (6oz) digestive biscuits
75g (3oz) butter, melted
25g (1oz) soft brown sugar
75g (3oz) pecan nut halves
225g (8oz) marshmallows
300ml (½ pint) strong black coffee
15g (½oz) gelatine
3 tablespoons hot water
150ml (5 fl oz) double cream
1 teaspoon ground coffee

Crush the biscuits and mix together with the butter and sugar.

Press the mixture onto the base and up the sides of an 18cm (7 inch) spring-form cake tin. Chill. Reserve 8 halves of pecan nuts for decoration and chop the remainder. In a large saucepan dissolve the marshmallows in the coffee, heating gently and stirring frequently. Dissolve the gelatine in the hot water and stir into the marshmallow mixture. Leave to cool until almost set. Whisk the cream until it peaks and fold into the coffee mixture. Add the chopped nuts. Pour onto the crushed biscuit base and chill until set. Remove from the tin and decorate with the nut halves. Sprinkle with the ground coffee.

Savarin Chantilly

PREPARATION TIME: 35 minutes
plus chilling

COOKING TIME: 30 minutes

OVEN: 200°C (400°F) Gas Mark 6

Savarin
150g (6oz) strong white flour
½ teaspoon salt
6 tablespoons milk
2 level teaspoons dried yeast
1 level teaspoon caster sugar
2 eggs
75g (3oz) butter

Syrup
150g (6oz) caster sugar
250ml (½ pint) water
Pared rind of ½ lemon and juice of 1 lemon
3 tablespoons rum

Filling
125ml (¼ pint) single cream
125ml (¼ pint) double cream
400g (1lb) tinned or fresh fruit

Savarin
Butter and sprinkle with flour a 20cm (8 inch) ring mould. Sift the flour and salt into a mixing bowl. Heat the milk in a small saucepan and add the dried yeast and sugar (do not boil the milk). Leave in a warm place for 20 minutes or until the mixture looks frothy. Mix the eggs into the yeast mixture and pour into the flour. Stir with a wooden spoon to form a smooth batter. Melt the butter and allow it to cool slightly. Pour into the batter and stir. Pour the batter into the ring mould and spread evenly. Put the mould into a polythene bag but leave room for the mixture to rise. Leave in a warm place. When the mixture has risen to the top of the tin bake in a preheated oven for half an hour until golden brown and firm to the touch.

Syrup
While the savarin is baking, add the sugar and water to a saucepan and finely pare the lemon rind. Stir over a low heat until the sugar has dissolved. Bring the mixture to the boil and simmer for 5 minutes. Remove from the heat and add the lemon juice and rum. When the savarin has cooled in the tin for five minutes remove it from the tin. Wash and dry the baking mould and pour the hot syrup evenly round the mould. Replace the savarin so that it floats in the syrup.

Filling
The savarin will soak up the syrup so that it can be turned out. Turn out the savarin and refrigerate overnight. Place savarin on a serving dish and whip the single and double cream. Spoon into the centre and top with fruit (apricot, mango, oranges or stoned cherries make a suitable decoration).

Mont Blanc

PREPARATION TIME: 20 minutes
plus chilling

COOKING TIME: 1¼ hours

OVEN: 120°C (250°F) Gas Mark ½

2 egg whites
185g (6oz) caster sugar
½ teaspoon vanilla essence
225ml (7½ fl oz) double cream
1½ tablespoons icing sugar
277g (8oz) can chestnut purée
1 tablespoon brandy
25g (1oz) plain chocolate, grated or chopped nuts

Whisk the egg whites until they peak, adding the sugar and vanilla essence. Fill a piping bag with the meringue mixture and fit a 1cm (½ inch) plain nozzle. Draw six circles 7.5cm (3 inches) diameter on a baking sheet lined with non-stick silicone paper and cover with the meringue. Bake in a very cool oven until firm but not brown. Cool. Whip the cream until it peaks and fold in the icing sugar. Mix the chestnut purée with the brandy and spoon the mixture into a piping bag fitted with a 3mm (⅛ inch) nozzle and pipe round the edge of the meringue bases. Top with cream and chocolate or nuts to decorate. Serve chilled.

Mango Soufflé

PREPARATION TIME: 20 minutes
plus chilling

1 tablespoon water
Juice of one lemon
75g (3oz) caster sugar
15g (½oz) gelatine
3 eggs (separated)
1 mango peeled and stoned
140ml (5 fl oz) double cream

To decorate
25g (1oz) toasted chopped nuts
140ml (5 fl oz) whipping cream, whipped
Caramel chips (see quick garnishes)

Prepare a 12.5cm (5 inch) freezerproof soufflé dish. Cut a double strip of lightly oiled greaseproof paper 50 x 12.5cm (20 x 5 inches) and tie securely round the dish. Put the water and lemon juice in a small pan and sprinkle in the gelatine. Heat to dissolve the gelatine and cool. Whisk the egg yolks and sugar until thick. Purée the mango and mix with the gelatine into the egg mixture. Fold in the stiffly whisked egg white with cream. Pour into the prepared dish and chill.

To decorate
Carefully remove the paper and press the nuts into the sides. Decorate with whipped cream. Another method of decoration is to use caramel chips.

Red Fruit Compote

PREPARATION TIME: 10 minutes
plus chilling

100g (4oz) granulated sugar
300ml (½ pint) water
150g (6oz) redcurrants, stalks
 removed
225g (8oz) raspberries, hulled
225g (8oz) strawberries, hulled
2 tablespoons Cointreau or orange
 liqueur
Single cream

Boil the sugar and water in a pan
till the sugar dissolves. This should
take about 5 minutes. Remove
from heat and cool. Put all the
fruits in a serving dish and pour
over the Cointreau and leave to
stand for an hour and a half. Stir
carefully from time to time. Pour
the cold syrup over the fruits and
serve chilled with cream.

Individual Fruit Salad

PREPARATION TIME: 20 minutes
plus chilling

3 bananas
2 oranges
100g (4oz) strawberries
50g (2oz) redcurrants

Passion Fruit Sauce
3 passion fruits
3 tablespoons clear honey
Juice of one lime
2 tablespoons dark rum

Peel and slice horizontally the bananas and oranges. Hull and halve the strawberries and arrange on individual plates and chill.

Passion Fruit Sauce
Spoon out the seeds and flesh of the passion fruits and boil with the honey and lime juice. Add two tablespoons of dark rum and chill. Pour the passion fruit sauce over the fruit and serve. Decorate with the redcurrants.

Almond Cream Flan

PREPARATION TIME: 20 minutes
COOKING TIME: 35 minutes
OVEN: 200°C (400°F) Gas Mark 6

Flan
50g (2oz) plain flour
50g (2oz) caster sugar
2 eggs

Filling
150ml (5 fl oz) double cream
1 level tablespoon sieved icing sugar
25g (1oz) ground almonds
350g (12oz) strawberries, hulled and sliced; keep one whole strawberry for decoration

Glaze
3 tablespoons water
75g (3oz) caster sugar
Whipped cream and strawberry leaves (optional)

Flan
Grease a 20cm (8 inch) flan tin. Line the base with a circle of greaseproof paper. Sieve the flour into a bowl. Put the caster sugar and eggs into another bowl and whisk for 12 minutes over a saucepan of hot water, off the heat. The mixture should thicken and pale. Remove from the pan and whisk for another 5 minutes. If using an electric whisk, omit the whisking over hot water. Sieve the flour a little at a time over the mixture and fold in with a metal spoon. Pour mixture into prepared tin and cook in a hot oven until firm. When cooked, leave to cool in the tin for a few minutes then turn onto a wire rack.

Filling
Whip the cream stiffly, adding the icing sugar slowly. Fold in the almonds and spoon this mixture into the flan base. Arrange the strawberries on top.

Glaze
Place water and sugar in a pan and slowly bring to the boil. The sugar should be dissolved. Stir the rapidly boiling mixture constantly. Boil for 2 minutes. Allow the glaze to cool and brush over the strawberries. Decorate with whipped cream and strawberry leaves if available.

Red Fruit Compote (far left), Individual Fruit Salad with Passion Fruit Sauce (centre) and Almond Cream Flan (left).

Petits Pots de Café

PREPARATION TIME: 10 minutes
plus cooling

3 tablespoons caster sugar
40g (1½oz) butter
1½ tablespoons rum
3 teaspoons instant coffee powder
  (granules should be crushed)
3 eggs, separated
120ml (4 fl oz) double cream,
  whipped
Walnut halves

Mix the sugar, butter, rum and
coffee in a bowl over a pan of hot
water, and stir until melted. Add
the egg yolks and mix well. Leave
to cook for 5 minutes over the hot
water and remove from the heat.
When the mixture has cooled,
whisk the egg whites until stiff and
fold into the coffee mixture. Spoon
into individual ranekins and
decorate with whipped cream and
nuts if available.

Fruit Coupelles with Dried Fruit Compote

PREPARATION TIME: 20 minutes
COOKING TIME: 7 minutes
OVEN: 200°C (400°F) Gas Mark 6

100g (4oz) dried apricots
50g (2oz) dried apple
100g (4oz) prunes
50g (2oz) raisins
50g (2oz) sultanas
50g (2oz) currants
500ml (1 pint) strong black coffee

Coupelles
2 egg whites
65g (2½oz) caster sugar
50g (2oz) plain flour
50g (2oz) butter, melted and cooled

Place all the fruit ingredients in a
saucepan and cover with the
coffee. Boil rapidly then reduce
heat to simmer for 3 minutes. Pour
into a bowl and leave to cool for at
least 10 hours. Whisk the egg
whites until frothy. Add the sugar
slowly. The mixture should be very
stiff. Fold in the flour and melted
butter. Grease a baking sheet. Drop
the mixture onto the baking sheet
to form 10cm (4 inch) rounds (the
mixture makes 8). Cook in a
preheated moderate oven until the
edges are golden brown. Remove
from the baking sheet one at a
time. Mould over an inverted
ramekin to form a cup shape.

When set remove from the dish
and leave to cool on a wire rack. To
serve fill the coupelles with the
fruit compote.

Loganberries and Hazelnut Galette

PREPARATION TIME: 35 minutes
COOKING TIME: 20 minutes
OVEN: 190°C (375°F) Gas Mark 5

100g (4oz) hazelnuts, shelled
100g (4oz) softened butter
75g (3oz) caster sugar
1 egg yolk, lightly beaten
A few drops of vanilla essence
150g (6oz) plain flour
A pinch of salt
150g (6oz) plain flour
425ml (15 fl oz) double cream
1 level tablespoon caster sugar
450g (1lb) loganberries, hulled

Lightly grease three baking trays
and dust with flour. Roast the
hazelnuts in a hot oven 220°C
(425°F) Gas Mark 7, or under the
grill until the skin is split. Rub off
the skins using kitchen paper and
chop the nuts finely. Whisk the
sugar and butter until fluffy and
beat in the egg yolk and vanilla
essence. Sieve the flour and salt
and stir into the mixture adding
the hazelnuts. Knead the mixture
till it forms a smooth dough. Wrap
in clear film and chill for 30
minutes. Divide the dough into 3
pieces and roll on a lightly floured
surface to form 17.5cm (7 inch)
rounds. Place each round onto the
previously greased baking sheet.
Cook one at a time in a moderately
heated oven until lightly golden.
Cut one round into 8 equal
portions while still hot and leave
the remaining 2 to cool for 10
minutes. Whip the cream until
thick and add the sugar. Put half
the mixture into a piping bag and
save eight loganberries for
decoration. Mix the remaining
berries with the cream. Carefully
position one galette on a serving
plate. Cover with loganberry cream
mixture and top with the
remaining galette. Pipe eight swirls
of cream on top and arrange the
galette triangles on their edges
supported by the cream swirls.
Decorate with the reserved
loganberries.

Pears in Wine

PREPARATION TIME: 15 minutes
plus chilling
COOKING TIME: 30 minutes

250g (12oz) granulated sugar
125ml (¼ pint) water
6 large pears, peeled
225ml (7½ fl oz) dry red wine

Gently heat the sugar and water
until the sugar has dissolved. Add
the pears and cover. Then simmer
for 15 minutes. Stir in the wine and
continue to simmer uncovered for
another 15 minutes. Remove the
pears from the saucepan and
arrange in a serving dish. Bring the
wine syrup back to the boil until
thick. Pour over the pears and
allow to cool. Serve chilled.

Strawberry and Peach Heart

PREPARATION TIME: 20 minutes
plus chilling

3 passion fruit
4 fl oz white wine
75g (3oz) caster sugar
3 tablespoons Cointreau or orange
  liqueur
100g (4oz) strawberries, hulled
3 peaches, halved and stoned
3 tablespoons strawberry jam
3 kumquats
3 kiwi fruit
3 tablespoons clear honey
1 teaspoon lime juice

Poach the flesh with the seeds of
the passion fruit in the white wine
until just tender. Add the sugar
and continue to poach for a further
four minutes. Sieve the mixture.
Add the Cointreau and the
strawberries and leave to cool. In a
large saucepan filled with boiling
water quickly submerge the

**This page: Mango Soufflé
(top), Mont Blanc (centre)
and Petits Pots de Café
(bottom).**

**Facing page: Loganberries
and Hazelnut Galette (top),
Fruit Coupelles with Dried
Fruit Salad (centre) and Pears
in Wine (bottom).**

peaches and halve, removing the stone. Sieve the strawberry jam and using a writing nozzle fill a piping bag, and reserve in the refrigerator. Slice the kumquats. To make the kiwi fruit sauce, peel the kiwi fruit and purée them. Pass them through a sieve and stir in the honey and lime juice. Using the sieved strawberry jam reserved in piping bag, pipe heart shapes on each of the individual plates making sure not to break the line of strawberry jam. Fill the outline with the fruit, placing the peach half to one side and fill the hole left by removing stone with the strawberries. Pour over the kiwi fruit sauce and decorate with leaves. Serve chilled.

Chocolate and Brandy Cheesecake

PREPARATION TIME: 30 minutes
plus chilling

COOKING TIME: 1 hour

OVEN: 160°C (325°F) Gas Mark 3

175g (6oz) plain chocolate digestives
75g (3oz) butter, melted
175g (6oz) plain chocolate
2 tablespoons brandy
2 eggs, lightly beaten
100g (4oz) soft brown sugar
350g (12oz) cream cheese
2 tablespoons cornflour

To decorate
Icing sugar

Crush the biscuits and mix them with the melted butter. Butter the sides and base of a loose-bottomed 18cm (7 inch) cake tin. Spoon the biscuit mixture into the cake tin, press onto the sides and base, and refrigerate for half an hour. Melt 100g (4oz) of the chocolate in a heatproof bowl over a pan of water and stir in the brandy. Beat together the eggs and sugar until thick. Add the cheese and continue to beat until the mixture is soft. Stir in the melted chocolate and cornflour. Pour the mixture into the cake tin and stand it on a baking sheet. Bake until it sets. Remove from the oven and cool, then chill for 4 hours before serving. To serve: remove the cheesecake from the cake tin and grate the remaining chocolate on top. Sift with a little icing sugar and serve.

Peach Brûlée

PREPARATION TIME: 20 minutes

GRILL SETTING: high

8 egg yolks
75g (3oz) caster sugar
1½ teaspoons vanilla essence
6 peach halves tinned or fresh
75g (3oz) soft brown sugar
Double cream

Beat the egg yolks and caster sugar until smooth and thick. Beat in the cream and pour the mixture into a saucepan. Cook over a low heat.

This page: Summer Pudding (left) and Strawberry and Peach Heart (right).

Facing page: Apricot Cream Cheese Dessert (top left), Peach Brûlée (top right) and Chocolate Brandy Cheesecake (bottom).

Stir frequently until the mixture is thick enough to coat the back of a wooden spoon. Beat for 2 minutes off the heat. Stir in the vanilla essence and pour the mixture into a heatproof serving dish. When cool, arrange the peach halves on top of the custard (cut side down). Chill for 1 hour. Sprinkle the soft brown sugar over the peaches and place the dish under a hot grill. When the sugar melts and starts to caramelise remove the dish from the grill and serve at once.

Summer Pudding

PREPARATION TIME: 10 minutes
plus chilling

750g (1lb 8oz) fresh soft fruit
175g (6oz) granulated sugar
9 slices of white bread (use thick
    slices and remove the crusts)
Whipped cream

Put all the fruit into a saucepan
with the sugar and heat until the
sugar is dissolved. Shake the pan so
that the fruit will stay whole.
Remove from heat and cool. Line
the base and sides of a 900ml (1½
pint) pudding basin with the slices
of bread trying not to leave any
gaps. Pour the fruit juice into the
centre of the pudding and cover
the top completely with bread and
press down firmly. Place a saucer or
small plate on top of the pudding
and weigh down. Chill in the fridge
overnight. Turn out and decorate
with whipped cream.

Almond Pear

PREPARATION TIME: 20 minutes
plus chilling

COOKING TIME: 1 hour

OVEN: 150°C (300°F) Gas Mark 2

600ml (1 pint) double cream
6 egg yolks
50g (2oz) caster sugar
½ teaspoon almond essence
100g (4oz) granulated sugar
150ml (¼ pint) water
4 large pears peeled, stoned and
    sliced thinly
175g (6oz) soft brown sugar
Lemon juice to sprinkle on pears

Pour the cream into a saucepan and
heat (do not allow the cream to
boil). Put the egg yolks, caster sugar
and almond essence into a bowl
and stir well. Slowly pour into the

heated cream. Pour the mixture
into a 900ml (1½ pint) baking dish
and stand the dish in a roasting tin
half filled with water (this is known
as a *bain marie*). Loosely cover with
foil and bake until set. Remove the
dish from the bain marie and leave
until cold. Refrigerate overnight.
Put the granulated sugar and water
in a saucepan and heat gently until
the sugar has dissolved. Bring to
the boil until thick and golden in
colour. Oil a shallow cake tin and
pour the caramelised sugar in.
When the caramel has set, crack
into small pieces with a rolling pin.
Arrange the pear slices on top of
the baked cream and sprinkle with
demerara sugar, and lemon juice.
Grill until the sugar has dissolved
and the juice is bubbling. Leave to
cool and return to the fridge for
half an hour. Sprinkle with caramel
chips before serving.

Apricot Cream Cheese Dessert

PREPARATION TIME: 20 minutes
plus chilling

GRILL SETTING: high

225g (8oz) crushed brandy snaps
½ teaspoon ground ginger
125g (4oz) butter, melted
450g (1lb) cream cheese
50g (2oz) caster sugar
125ml (4 fl oz) single cream
2 tablespoons lemon juice
1 tablespoon gelatine dissolved in
    2 tablespoons hot water
450g (1lb) can of apricot halves,
    drained
50g (2oz) preserved stem ginger,
    drained and chopped
40ml (15 fl oz) double cream
50g (2oz) soft brown sugar

Grease a 23cm (9 inch) loose-
bottomed cake tin with a little
butter. In a large mixing bowl crush

the brandy snaps, ground ginger
and butter and spoon into the base
of the cake tin, pressing down with
the back of a spoon. Place the
cream cheese and caster sugar into
a bowl and beat with a wooden
spoon until the mixture is smooth.
Stir in the single cream, lemon juice
and dissolved gelatine. Beat well so
that all the mixture is blended
together. Spoon the mixture into
the tin and refrigerate for 40
minutes. When the filling is set,
remove the tin and arrange the
apricot halves on top of the filling.
Sprinkle over the preserved ginger
and soft brown sugar. Grill for
three minutes until the sugar has
caramelised. Remove the dessert
from the tin and serve.

Orange and Lemon Chiffon Flan

PREPARATION TIME: 45 minutes

COOKING TIME: 20 minutes

OVEN: 200°C (400°F) Gas Mark 6

Pastry Case
175g (6oz) plain flour
Pinch of salt
90g (3½oz) butter
25g (1oz) caster sugar
1 egg yolk

Filling
3 eggs, separated
75g (3oz) caster sugar
2 large oranges
1 large lemon
1 tablespoon gelatine
Warm water

For decoration
Sliced orange and lemon fan
150ml (5 fl oz) whipped cream

Pastry Case
Sieve the flour and salt into a bowl
and rub in the fat. Add the sugar
and mix well. Mix to a stiff paste
with the egg yolk to form a pliable

dough. Turn onto a floured board
and roll out. Use to line a 20cm (8
inch) flan ring. Cut a circle from
non-stick silicone baking paper and
lay on top of pastry. Sprinkle with
baking beans or crusts of bread
(baking blind). Bake for about 20
minutes at 200°C (400°F) Gas
Mark 6. Remove the baking beans
and paper and return to the oven
for 5 minutes.

Filling
Whisk the egg yolks, sugar and
grated rind of two oranges and one
lemon until thick. Dissolve the
gelatine in a little warm water and
make up to 300ml (½ pint) with
orange juice and water. Pour the
gelatine mixture into the egg
mixture and whisk until it starts to
thicken. Lightly fold in the stiffly
beaten egg white, pile into the flan
case and leave to set. Decorate
with whipped cream and slices of
orange.

Gateau American

PREPARATION TIME: 10 minutes

COOKING TIME: 20 minutes

OVEN: 200°C (400°F) Gas Mark 6

75g (3oz) granulated sugar
10g (½ oz) butter
75g (3oz) breadcrumbs
3 eggs, beaten
300g (¾lb) stoned dates
75g (3oz) walnuts, chopped
450ml (15 fl oz) whipped cream
    (whipping or double)
Nuts

Mix the sugar, butter and breadcrumbs with the beaten eggs, dates
and walnuts. Cook in a shallow
pan until cooked (20 minutes).
When cold, crumble with a fork.
Layer fruit mixture and stiffly
whipped cream in tall glasses and
top with a rosette of whipped
cream. Decorate with a nut.

**Facing page: Almond Pear (top), Gateau
American (right) and Orange and Lemon
Chiffon Flan (bottom).**

Summer Desserts

Gooseberry Pie

PREPARATION TIME: 20 minutes

COOKING TIME: 1 hour

OVEN: 220°C (425°F) Gas Mark 7 for 30 minutes, then 180°C (350°F) Gas Mark 4 for 30 minutes

Pastry
275g (10oz) plain flour
Pinch of salt
65g (2½oz) butter (cut into small pieces)
65g (2½oz) lard (cut into small pieces)
2½ tablespoons cold water

Filling
900g (2lb) gooseberries, topped and tailed
225g (8oz) granulated sugar
Milk to glaze or beaten egg
Single cream or custard

Pastry
Sift the flour with the salt. Add the fat and mix until it resembles breadcrumbs. Stir in the water and form into a firm dough. Roll out half the pastry on a lightly floured surface and use it to line a 20cm (8 inch) flan dish or pie dish.

Filling
Mix the gooseberries with the sugar and fill the lined pastry dish. Roll out the remaining pastry and cover the pie. Dampen the edges and seal together. Any excess pastry can be used to make leaves to decorate. Make a small hole in the centre of the pie and brush the pastry with milk or beaten egg. Place on baking tray and cook in a hot oven. Serve with single cream or custard.

Melons and Mangoes on Ice

PREPARATION TIME: 1¼ hours

1 medium size Ogen melon
2 large mangoes

Slice melon in half and scoop out flesh in balls. Peel mangoes and slice. Mix mango slices and melon balls together and arrange in a glass bowl. Chill for 1 hour.

Frozen Gooseberry Fool

PREPARATION TIME: 20 minutes plus freezing

COOKING TIME: 15 minutes

650g (1½lb) gooseberries
450ml (¾ pint) water
Sprig of mint
150g (6 oz) caster sugar
A little green food colouring
450ml (¾ pint) double cream, lightly whipped

Top and tail gooseberries. Place in a pan with the water and mint. Cover and simmer for approximately 15 minutes or until soft. Take off the heat and stir in the sugar until dissolved, then add food colouring. Take out the sprig of mint. Sieve and ensure all pips are removed. Cool and blend with the cream. Place in container and freeze.

Brown Bread Ice Cream

PREPARATION TIME: 20 minutes plus freezing

475ml (17 fl oz) vanilla ice cream
4 small slices brown bread
1 teaspoon ground cinnamon
125ml (4 fl oz) water
75g (3oz) sugar

Put the ice cream into a large mixing bowl and break it up, allowing it to soften. Cut the crusts from the bread and discard. Crumble the slices into a bowl, adding the ground cinnamon, reserve. Put the water and sugar into a small saucepan and stir until the sugar has dissolved. Boil until the mixture caramelises and turns brown. Remove from the heat and stir in the breadcrumbs and cinnamon mixture. Blend the mixture into the ice cream, making sure the breadcrumbs do not form large lumps. Turn the mixture into a rigid container for freezing, (leave 10mm (½ inch) space at the top of the container). Freeze the mixture and serve.

Brown Bread Ice Cream (top left), Melons and Mangoes on Ice (top right), Frozen Gooseberry Fool (bottom left) and Gooseberry Pie (bottom right).

Cherry 'Spoom'

PREPARATION TIME: 20 minutes
plus freezing

250g (9oz) sugar
300ml (½ pint) water
Juice of 2 limes
2 fresh peppermint leaves
600ml (1 pint) Sauternes
3 egg whites
Cherry brandy

Boil 100g (4oz) of the sugar with
the water, lime juice and
peppermint leaves. Leave to cool
and strain into the Sauternes.
Freeze the sorbet. Whisk the egg
whites and add the remaining sugar
until it peaks. Remove the sorbet
from the freezer and whisk in the
meringue mixture. Serve in glasses
and pour over the cherry brandy.

Apple and Sultana and Brandy Ice

PREPARATION TIME: 10 minutes
plus soaking and freezing time

600ml (1 pint) apple juice
50g (2oz) caster sugar
42g (1½oz) packet dried apple flakes
100g (4oz) sultanas
A few drops green food colour
1 egg white, stiffly whisked

Put the apple juice in a pan with
sugar. Heat gently until the sugar
has dissolved. Boil quickly for 5
minutes and remove from heat.
Cool. Soak apple flakes and
sultanas in brandy and add enough
apple syrup to cover mixture. Soak
for 4 hours. Then mix apple,
sultanas and brandy adding a few
drops of food colour mixture with
the remaining apple syrup in a
shallow container and freeze. Mash
with a fork and fold in egg whites.
Return to the freezer. Serve frozen
in glasses.

This page: **Burgundy Granita
(top), Apple and Sultana and
Brandy Ice (centre) and
Champagne Granita
(bottom).**

Facing page: **Cherry 'Spoom'
(top), Raspberry Malakoff
(centre) and Cherry
Cinnamon Sorbet (bottom).**

Burgundy Granita

PREPARATION TIME: 15 minutes
plus freezing

75g (3oz) sugar, plus 2 tablespoons
Juice of ½ lime and ½ orange
1 tablespoon water
Small bunch lemon balm leaves
½ bottle good Burgundy
125ml (4 fl oz) double or whipping
   cream
Blackberries to decorate

Boil half the sugar with the lime and orange juice and water, and the balm leaves. Cool, strain and add to Burgundy. Freeze in a shallow container. To serve: whip the cream with the remaining sugar. Scrape the granita with a spoon to produce ice shavings and serve shavings into glasses, decorate with cream and blackberries.

Champagne Granita

PREPARATION TIME: 5 minutes
plus freezing time

⅔ bottle champagne
Fresh blackcurrants and raspberries
Caster sugar to dust

Freeze the champagne in a shallow container. When frozen, scrape off and serve into glasses. Decorate with blackcurrants and raspberries. Dust with caster sugar.

Raspberry Malakoff

PREPARATION TIME: 35 minutes
plus chilling

175g (6oz) caster sugar
175g (6oz) butter
300ml (½ pint) double cream
175g (6oz) ground almonds
3 tablespoons kirsch
225g (8oz) fresh raspberries
1 packet boudoir biscuits
Whipped cream

Beat the sugar and butter until fluffy. Whip the cream until it peaks and fold in the ground almonds. Add the kirsch and raspberries. Mix the sugar and butter with the cream fruit mixture. Line an 18cm (7 inch) cake tin with non-stick silicone paper. Stand the boudoir biscuits round the sides of the cake tin with the sugary side outermost. Spoon the malakoff mixture into the middle and press it down. Make sure the top is smooth. Refrigerate until the malakoff feels firm. With a sharp knife, trim the biscuits to the same level as the malakoff mixture. Turn the malakoff out upside down. Decorate with whipped cream if desired. Serve chilled.

Cherry Cinnamon Sorbet

PREPARATION TIME: 25 minutes
plus freezing

175g (10oz) sugar, plus 1 tablespoon
300ml (½ pint) water
1 piece cinnamon stick
500g (18oz) fresh sour cherries
Juice of ½ lemon
200ml (7 fl oz) whipping cream
Seeds of ¼ vanilla pod
Fresh cherries

Boil 175g (10oz) of the sugar for 3 minutes in water and cinnamon and leave to cool. Remove the cinnamon sticks and stone the cherries. Purée the cherries and stir in the lemon juice. Mix with the sugar syrup and freeze. Flavour the cream with the tablespoon of sugar and vanilla. Whip until thick. Put the sorbet into individual glasses and decorate with cream and cherries.

Strawberry Alaska

PREPARATION TIME: 10 minutes
COOKING TIME: 2-3 minutes
OVEN: 140°C (275°F) Gas Mark 1

1 shop-bought strawberry jam swiss
   roll
Soft-scoop strawberry ice cream to
   cover

Meringue
2 egg whites
100g (4oz) caster sugar

Cover swiss roll with ice cream. Return to freezer. Whisk egg whites until they form stiff peaks. Whisk in half the sugar. Then fold in the rest. Remove ice cream covered swiss roll from freezer and cover with meringue mixture. Place in oven and cook meringue until just turning golden. (Approximately 2-3 minutes.) Serve immediately.

Strawberry Yogurt Ice

PREPARATION TIME: 20 minutes
plus freezing

225g (8oz) fresh or thawed, frozen
   strawberries
300ml (½ pint) plain low fat yogurt
2 teaspoons gelatine
2 tablespoons water
1 egg white
65g (2½oz) caster sugar
A few strawberries

Blend strawberries and yogurt until smooth. Sprinkle gelatine over the water in a small bowl. Place bowl in a pan of hot water until the gelatine is dissolved. Cool slightly and add to the strawberry mixture. Pour into the container and freeze until icy round the edges. Put mixture into bowl and beat until smooth. In another bowl whisk the egg white stiffly, carefully adding the sugar and fold into strawberry mixture. Pour back into container and freeze. To serve – scoop into glasses and decorate with strawberries.

Peach Melba

PREPARATION TIME: 10 minutes

1 large can peaches (2 halves per
   person)
2 scoops ice cream per person
Chocolate sauce or raspberry purée
Flaked almonds

Place 2 scoops of ice cream per serving in individual bowls. Place 2 peach halves on top. Serve with chocolate sauce or raspberry purée. Decorate with flaked almonds.

Lemon Sorbet

PREPARATION TIME: 15 minutes
plus freezing

Grated rinds and juice of 2 lemons
Cold water
75g (3oz) caster sugar
1 teaspoon gelatine
2 egg whites

Mix the lemon juice and rind with cold water to make 1 litre (1¾ pints) of fluid. Put the liquid in a saucepan with the sugar and boil. Remove from the heat and whisk in the gelatine. Pour into a mixing bowl and place in the freezer until it begins to harden. Whisk the egg whites until stiff and beat them into the lemon mixture. Return to the freezer, leaving a 10mm (½ inch) head space in the container.

Pastel Coupé

PREPARATION TIME: 35 minutes
plus freezing

Yellow
600ml (1 pint) water
2 level teaspoons gelatine
250g (10oz) caster sugar
3 lemons
2 egg whites

Green
600ml (1 pint) water
2 level teaspoons gelatine
200g (8oz) caster sugar
2 lemons
2 egg whites
2 tablespoons crème de menthe

Yellow
Measure out two tablespoons of water and sprinkle with gelatine. Place the remaining water and sugar in a saucepan. Add pared lemon rinds and stir over the heat until the sugar has dissolved. Bring to the boil and simmer for 5 minutes. Remove from heat and add gelatine mixture. Dissolve completely and stir in the lemon juice. Leave to cool. Strain the mixture into a container and freeze until partially frozen. Place in chilled mixing bowl and whisk with beaten egg whites until thick and snowy. Return to container and freeze.

Green
For the green pastel coupé use basic method and ingredients as listed. Add the crème de menthe with lemon juice. To serve: use an ice-cream scoop, take half the green and half the yellow into one scoop. Serve in meringue cases or glasses.

Facing page: Strawberry Yogurt Ice (top), Peach Melba (centre) and Strawberry Alaska (bottom).

Curaçao Granita with Champagne

PREPARATION TIME: 10 minutes
plus freezing

75g (3oz) sugar
150ml (¼ pint) water
Juice of 1 lime
Juice of 1 orange
3 tablespoons blue Curaçao
⅔ bottle champagne

Boil half the sugar with the water, lime and orange juice for two to three minutes. Cool, strain, add to the Curaçao and the champagne. Pour into a flat freezer-proof container and freeze. To serve: scrape with a spoon and serve in glasses.

Blackcurrant Sorbet

PREPARATION TIME: 20 minutes
plus freezing

1kg (2lb) fresh or thawed, frozen
   blackcurrants
225g (9oz) sugar
300ml (½ pint) water
2 egg whites

Put all the ingredients except the egg whites into a saucepan. Heat slowly and cook for 15 minutes. Rub the fruit mixture through a sieve and pour into a freezer-proof container with a lid. Freeze until mushy. Whisk the egg whites until firm and fold into the mixture. Return to the freezer.

Inset illustration: (from top to bottom) Curaçao Granita with Champagne, Lemon Sorbet, Pastel Coupé and Blackcurrant Sorbet.

Ginger Syllabub

PREPARATION TIME: 15 minutes

1 100g (4oz) jar preserved ginger
600ml (1 pint) double cream, lightly
whipped

Chop 2 pieces of the ginger and mix into the cream along with 2 tablespoons of the syrup. Serve in glasses or bowls and decorate with sliced ginger. Chill until ready to serve.

Apricot Ice Roll

PREPARATION TIME: 35 minutes
plus freezing

COOKING TIME: 12 minutes

OVEN: 220°C (425°F) Gas Mark 7

Sponge mixture
2 eggs
50g (2oz) caster sugar
50g (2oz) plain flour

Filling and decorating
4 tablespoons apricot jam
600ml (1 pint) soft-scoop ice cream
(vanilla)
Cream to decorate
Dried apricots, thinly sliced

Whisk eggs and sugar until light and fluffy. Carefully fold in flour. Turn into a greased and floured swiss roll tin and bake. Turn out onto a tea towel and leave to cool. Spread sponge with apricot jam and softened ice cream. Roll up using tea towel. Place in freezer until ice cream is hardened. Decorate with cream and sliced apricots.

Mango Sorbet

PREPARATION TIME: 15 minutes
plus freezing

250ml (8 fl oz) mango purée
Juice of ½ lime
Scant 150ml (5 fl oz) dry white wine
Scant 150ml (5 fl oz) mineral water
1 egg white
50g (2oz) sugar

Mix the mango purée with the lime juice, white wine and mineral water. Whisk the egg white until it peaks and slowly add the sugar. Fold the egg white into the mango mixture and freeze.

Apricot Ice Roll (far left), Ginger Syllabub (centre) and Mango Sorbet (left).

Banana Ice Crêpes

PREPARATION TIME: 30 minutes

12 cooked crêpes
2 large bananas
12 scoops soft-scoop vanilla ice
    cream
Chocolate sauce

Mash one banana, and combine with ice cream. Fold the crêpes in half and place on individual plates. Fill crêpes with the mixture of banana and ice cream. Decorate with other sliced banana. Serve with chocolate sauce.

Mousse Glacée au Chocolat

PREPARATION TIME: 20 minutes
plus freezing

4 egg yolks
2 tablespoons caster sugar
2 teaspoons vanilla essence
300ml (½ pint) double cream
2 egg whites, stiffly whipped
Chocolate sauce

Whisk egg yolks and sugar until light and creamy. Add vanilla essence. Add the cream and egg whites. Freeze the mixture. Serve with chocolate sauce.

Chocolate Banana Ice

PREPARATION TIME: 35 minutes
plus freezing

150ml (¼ pint) milk
40g (1½oz) caster sugar
40g (1½oz) plain chocolate (broken
    into bits)
1 egg, beaten
½ teaspoon vanilla essence
150ml (¼ pint) double cream,
    whipped until soft peaking

Banana Cream
4 medium bananas
1 tablespoon lemon juice
25g (1oz) icing sugar, sieved
150ml (¼ pint) whipped double
    cream

Place the milk, sugar and chocolate in a saucepan and heat gently. Pour onto the beaten egg and stir constantly until mixed. Return the mixture to the saucepan and cook until the custard thickens. Strain

the mixture, add the vanilla essence and allow to cool. Fold the cream into the custard mixture. Whisk rapidly and turn into a metal freezing container.

Banana Cream
Peel and chop the bananas and sprinkle with lemon juice. Dust the fruit with icing sugar and fold the whipped cream in with the bananas. Stir the chocolate mixture with banana cream and freeze. Remove from freezer to fridge 20 minutes before serving.

Refreshing Sorbet

PREPARATION TIME: 15 minutes
plus freezing

75g (3oz) caster sugar
425ml (¾ pint) water
3 ripe mangoes, peeled, stoned and
    mashed
Juice of 3 lemons
3 tablespoons white rum
3 egg whites, whisked

Over low heat, dissolve sugar in the water, boil for 10 minutes. Leave to cool. Blend mangoes with lemon juice and rum. Add the syrup. Pour into a container and freeze until just frozen. Turn into a bowl. Fold in the egg whites. Freeze.

Minted Lime Ice

PREPARATION TIME: 15 minutes
plus freezing

175g (6oz) caster sugar
375ml (12 fl oz) water
Grated rind and juice of 6 limes
4 tablespoons fresh mint, finely
    chopped
150ml (5 fl oz) double cream
3 tablespoons single cream

Place the sugar and water in a saucepan. Stir gently over a low heat. When the sugar has dissolved bring the mixture to the boil. Remove the pan from the heat. Stir in the grated rind of the limes. Add the juice and stir in the mint. Let the mixture cool and pour into ice trays. Freeze the mixture, covered with foil. When the mixture is frozen, crush it. Lightly whip the creams together. Stir the lime ice into the cream and re-freeze. Slightly thaw and spoon into small glasses to serve.

Lemon Ice Cream Sponge

PREPARATION TIME: 20 minutes
plus freezing
COOKING TIME: 15 minutes
OVEN: 220°C (425°F) Gas Mark 7

Sponge
3 large eggs
75g (3oz) caster sugar
75g (3oz) self raising flour, sieved

Filling
4 level teaspoons lemon curd
1 grated rind of lemon
6 scoops soft-scoop vanilla ice cream

To decorate
3 tablespoons double cream
Icing sugar
Sugared lemon slices

Sponge
Whisk eggs and sugar until light and fluffy. Sieve in flour and mix in carefully. Bake in a large 13cm (5 inch) baking tin. Turn out and cool.

Filling
Slice the cake into three horizontally. On bottom and middle slices spread lemon curd. Mix together the lemon rind and vanilla ice cream. Spread on top of the lemon curd. Sandwich together and freeze.

To decorate
Whip cream until stiff; place in piping bag with a star nozzle; pipe rosettes on top of the sponge. Dust with icing sugar and add lemon slices.

Custard Ice Cream

PREPARATION TIME: 20 minutes

5 egg yolks
150ml (¼ pint) single cream
150g (6oz) caster sugar
300ml (½ pint) double cream

Combine egg yolks, single cream and 100g (4oz) of the sugar in a basin. Place over a pan of simmering water and stir until mixture coats the back of a spoon. Strain mixture into a bowl and leave to cool. Whip double cream lightly. Mix with custard carefully. Fold in remaining 50g (2oz) of sugar. Pour into a freezer-proof container. Cover and freeze.

Coconut Sorbet

PREPARATION TIME: 20 minutes
plus freezing

250ml (8 fl oz) tinned coconut juice
Scant 150ml (5 fl oz) mineral water
2 tablespoons dark rum
2 egg whites
100g (4oz) sugar

To decorate
2 bananas, sliced
Chocolate sauce

Mix the coconut juice with the mineral water and rum. Whisk the egg whites until stiff, gradually adding the sugar. Stir the egg whites into the coconut mixture with a balloon whisk and freeze until creamy. Serve with banana slices and chocolate sauce.

Honey Ice Cream

PREPARATION TIME: 15 minutes
plus freezing

450g (1lb) raspberries
150ml (5 fl oz) clear honey
150ml (5 fl oz) double cream
2 tablespoons lemon juice
3 egg whites
120ml (4 fl oz) water
150ml (5 fl oz) single cream
4 x 15ml tablespoons granulated
    sugar

Cook the raspberries in a saucepan with the honey and water. Add the sugar and cook for 5 minutes until dissolved. Leave to cool. Rub the mixture through a sieve and chill. Beat the double cream until thick and stir in the single cream. Fold the creams into the fruit mixture. Freeze until almost solid. Whisk and re-freeze.

Facing page: Mocha Soufflé (top), Chocolate Banana Ice (centre left), Banana Ice Crêpes (centre right) and Mousse Glacée au Chocolat (bottom).

Fancy Ice

| **PREPARATION TIME:** 15 minutes |
| **COOKING TIME:** 10 minutes |
| **OVEN:** 220°C (425°F) Gas Mark 7 |

Sponge
2 eggs
50g (2oz) caster sugar
50g (2oz) flour

Topping
200g (8oz) fondant icing
1 tablespoon lemon juice
A few drops yellow food colour

Filling and decoration
Blackberry sorbet
Apricot purée
Blackberries

Sponge
Whisk eggs and caster sugar until light and fluffy. Sieve in the flour, fold gently into mixture. Lightly grease and flour a bun tin. Spoon into 12 portions and bake until golden brown. Turn out and cool on a wire rack.

Topping
Melt the fondant icing. Add the lemon juice and food colouring. Spoon over the cakes, leave to harden and set.

Filling and decoration
Fit a star nozzle on a piping bag and fill with blackberry sorbet. Cut the sponges in half and pipe onto top of base of cake; top with another. Serve with a spoonful of apricot purée on the side and decorate with blackberries.

Mocha Soufflé

| **PREPARATION TIME:** 30 minutes |
| plus chilling |

15g (½oz) gelatine
4 tablespoons warm water
25g (1oz) cocoa
1 teaspoon instant coffee
450ml (¾ pint) milk
4 eggs, separated
75g (3oz) caster sugar
2 tablespoons rum
150ml (5 fl oz) fresh double cream, whipped
Chocolate curls

Dissolve the gelatine in a small basin with the warm water. Mix the cocoa and coffee with the milk and bring to the boil in a saucepan. In a

mixing bowl beat the egg yolks and sugar together until pale and fluffy. Gradually beat in the milk mixture. Place the bowl over a saucepan of hot water for 15 minutes. Stir gently. Remove from heat and stir in the rum and dissolved gelatine. Allow to cool. Whisk the egg whites until they peak and fold into

the mixture. Mix in half of the double cream. Pour into a prepared ½ litre (1 pint) soufflé dish. Chill until set. Decorate with the remaining whipped cream and chocolate curls.

This page: Fancy Ice (top), Custard Ice Cream (centre) and Coconut Sorbet (bottom). Facing page: Refreshing Sorbet (top), Minted Lime Ice (centre left), Honey Ice Cream (centre right) and Lemon Ice Cream Sponge (bottom).

AutumnDesserts

Illustrations below: Charlotte (left), Steamed Chocolate Pudding with Rum Sauce (centre) and Viennoise Pudding with German Sauce (right).

Charlotte

PREPARATION TIME: 30 minutes

COOKING TIME: 40 minutes

OVEN: 180°C (350°F) Gas Mark 4

450g (1lb) cooking apples
100g (4oz) white breadcrumbs
50g (2oz) shredded suet
75g (3oz) brown sugar
1 lemon
Caster sugar for topping
Custard or cream

Wash, peel, core and slice the apples. Mix together the breadcrumbs, suet, sugar and grated lemon rind. Sprinkle a little of this mixture in the bottom of a greased pie dish. Then add a layer of apple slices (sprinkled with juice from the lemon) and fill the dish with alternate layers of the breadcrumb mixture and sliced apples – finishing with a layer of breadcrumbs. Bake in the oven for 40 minutes. Turn out onto a hot dish and sprinkle lightly with caster sugar. Serve with custard or cream.

Steamed Chocolate Pudding with Rum Sauce

PREPARATION TIME: 25 minutes

COOKING TIME: 1½ hours or until firm to touch

75g (3oz) plain cooking chocolate
Few drops of vanilla essence
75g (3oz) butter
150g (6oz) caster sugar
3 eggs
250g (9oz) self-raising flour
7½ tablespoons milk

Sauce
3 tablespoons cornflour
¾ pint milk
3 tablespoons sugar
3 tablespoons dark rum

Put the chocolate, vanilla and butter in a heatproof bowl placed over a pan of hot water. Heat gently, stirring to melt the chocolate and butter. When melted remove from the heat and cool. Stir the sugar into the chocolate mixture and beat in the eggs. Sift the flour and mix in well. Stir in the milk. Grease a 1.2 litre (2 pint) pudding basin. Pour the mixture into the pudding basin. Cover with a foil lid tied on securely with string. Steam pudding for 1½ hours.

Sauce
In a saucepan dissolve the cornflour in the milk. Stir in the sugar and heat gently, stirring constantly. Bring the mixture to the boil and then reduce heat and simmer until it thickens and is smooth. Stir in the rum. Turn out the pudding and serve hot with sauce.

Viennoise Pudding with German Sauce

PREPARATION TIME: 60 minutes

COOKING TIME: 90 minutes

25g (1oz) sugar cubes
1 tablespoon water
300ml (½ pint) milk
150g (6oz) bread
Grated rind of 1 lemon
75g (3oz) sultanas
40g (1½oz) chopped candied peel
3 eggs
½ wineglass of sherry
75g (3oz) caster sugar

Sauce
2 egg yolks
¼ pint sherry
12g (½oz) caster sugar
Strips of lemon rind

Using a thick pan, dissolve the sugar in a tablespoonful of water. Heat gently until dissolved, then bring to the boil and boil rapidly until the syrup turns brown. Heat the milk and pour over the syrup. Remove the crusts from the bread, then cut the bread into small cubes. Add the lemon rind, sultanas and candied peel. Beat the eggs and add the milk/syrup mixture to the eggs. Then add the sherry and caster sugar. Pour the whole mixture over the bread and leave to soak for 30 minutes. Transfer to a greased basin, cover with greased foil and steam for 60-90 minutes until firm.

Sauce

Beat the egg yolks, warm the sherry and then mix together with the sugar and lemon rind. Sit the basin in a pan of hot water and whisk thoroughly for 10 minutes. Do not over-heat the sauce or it will curdle. Serve immediately.

Crêpes

100g (4oz) plain flour
Pinch of salt or sugar (for extra
    sweetness)
1 egg, lightly beaten
300ml (½ pint) milk
1 teaspoon vegetable oil

Before doing any of the following pancake recipes, follow these instructions for making the crêpes. This mixture makes 12 crêpes. You can also buy them ready made.

Sieve the flour and salt into a bowl. Make a well in the centre and break an egg into it with half the milk. Beat well, then when smooth add the remaining milk. Leave the mixture to stand for 40 minutes. Grease the frying pan (or skillet) and heat it a little. Pour the batter into the pan. Quickly tilt and rotate the pan so the batter coats the bottom of the frying pan and pour off the excess batter. Cook over a moderate heat until the underside of the crêpe is gently brown. Turn crêpe over and brown the other side. Turn onto greaseproof paper and keep warm.

"Sissi" Crêpes

PREPARATION TIME: 25 minutes	
COOKING TIME: 20 minutes	
OVEN: 200°C (400°F) Gas Mark 6	

150g (6oz) almond paste
3 tablespoons sugar syrup
3 tablespoons lemon juice
1½ tablespoons kirsch
25g (1oz) softened butter
6 tablespoons strawberry sauce
6 tablespoons Advocaat
6 scoops vanilla ice cream
Whipped cream

Mix the almond paste with the sugar syrup, lemon juice and kirsch and beat until fluffy. Divide the mixture between the crêpes and roll or fold them. Spread with butter, put in ovenproof dish and

heat through at oven temperature 200°C (400°F) Gas Mark 6 for five minutes. Put them on small plates and pour over strawberry sauce and liqueur. Serve with whipped cream and vanilla ice cream.

Chocolate Crêpes

OVEN: 200°C (400°F) Gas Mark 6	

150g (6oz) cherry jam
125g (5oz) softened butter
150ml (¼ pint) water
125g (5oz) sugar
40g (1½oz) cocoa powder
3 tablespoons rum
150g (6oz) plain chocolate, chopped
6 tablespoons whipped cream

Fill the crêpes with the jam and roll or fold them. Spread them on top with half of the butter. Heat the crêpes for 5 minutes.

Sauce

In a saucepan boil up the water, sugar and the rest of the butter. Remove the pan from the heat and stir in the rum and chocolate. If the sauce is too thick, thin with single cream. Pour the hot sauce over the crêpes. Decorate with whipped cream.

Crêpes Suzette

PREPARATION TIME: 40 minutes	
COOKING TIME: 35 minutes	

Rind of 1 orange
6 lumps sugar
60g (2¼ oz) butter
100g (4oz) more sugar
150ml (6 fl oz) fresh orange juice
5 tablespoons orange liqueur
3 tablespoons brandy

Cream the 100g (4oz) sugar and the butter till fluffy. Beat in the orange juice and rub the sugar cubes onto the rind so they look orange, reserve. Add the orange liqueur gradually. Spoon a little of the mixture into each pancake and roll or fold. Put the remaining mixture into a large frying pan and place the crêpes on top. Scatter the sugar cubes on the top. Gently heat the pan and melt the butter. In another saucepan warm the brandy and pour over the pancakes. Ignite the brandy and serve.

Pear and Nut Crêpes

PREPARATION TIME: 25 minutes	
COOKING TIME: 15 minutes	
OVEN: 180°C (350°F) Gas Mark 4	

12 cooked crêpes
150g (6oz) butter
75g (3oz) icing sugar
75g (3oz) ground almonds
Few drops of almond essence
Grated rind of 1 lemon
650g (26oz) of tinned pears, drained
    and sliced

Cream the butter and sugar together till the mixture is fluffy. Beat the ground almonds, almond essence and lemon rind into the mixture. Fold the pears carefully into the mixture. Divide the mixture between the crêpes and roll or fold each one. Arrange the crêpes in an ovenproof dish and re-heat gently in a moderate oven. Serve hot.

Apple and Nut Tart

PREPARATION TIME: 20 minutes	
COOKING TIME: 40 minutes	
OVEN: 220°C (425°F) Gas Mark 7	

250g (9oz) flour
150g (5oz) sugar
Salt
1 egg
125g (4½oz) butter, cut into pieces

Filling

450g (1lb) dessert apples, peeled,
    cored and sliced
50g (2oz) ground hazelnuts
1 teaspoon ground cinnamon
Juice of 1 lemon
3 tablespoons apricot brandy
    (optional)
100g (4oz) apricot jam
50g (2oz) chopped nuts

Pastry

Sift the flour and sugar (reserving 25g (1oz) of sugar for filling) and a pinch of salt into a mixing bowl. Make a well in the centre and add the egg. Mix in the butter pieces, rub the ingredients to make a soft smooth dough. Rest the dough by leaving it in the fridge for 30 minutes. Grease a 20cm (8 inch) pie dish. Roll out the pastry, line the dish.

Filling

Layer the apple and hazelnuts. Sprinkle with cinnamon and sugar,

lemon juice and apricot brandy. Put the apricot jam in a saucepan and heat until melted. Pour over filling. Sprinkle with the chopped nuts. Bake until golden and fruit is soft. Take tart out of oven and cool.

Treacle Tart

PREPARATION TIME: 25 minutes	
COOKING TIME: 30 minutes	
OVEN: 180°C (350°F) Gas Mark 4	

Pastry

150g (6oz) plain flour
Pinch of salt
30g (1½oz) butter or margarine
30g (1½oz) lard
Cold water to mix

Filling

225g (8oz) golden syrup
50g (2oz) breadcrumbs
Lemon juice

Sieve the flour into a bowl. Add the salt and the lard to the flour. Chop the lard into small pieces with a knife and then rub into the flour with the fingertips. Add the water and mix to a stiff dough. Turn on to a lightly floured board and knead the dough until free from cracks. Roll out a little larger than a 23cm (9 inch) tin. Line the edge of the tin with a strip of pastry (cut from the edge). Damp it well and then line the whole tin with the rolled out pastry. Seal the edges, trim off any excess pastry and decorate the edges.

Filling

Sprinkle the breadcrumbs into the lined tin and cover with golden syrup. Add a little lemon juice. Cut the remaining pastry trimmings into thin strips, twist, and lay across the tart. Bake for 30 minutes.

Facing page: Pear and Nut Crêpes (top left), Crêpes Suzette (top right), Chocolate Crêpes (centre) and "Sissi" Crêpes (bottom).

Cherry Clafoutis

PREPARATION TIME: 15 minutes

COOKING TIME: 15 minutes

OVEN: 180°C (350°F) Gas Mark 4

350ml (12 fl oz) milk
1 tablespoon dark rum
4 eggs
100g (4oz) caster sugar
100g (4oz) flour
Generous pinch of salt
400g (14oz) stoned cherries
Icing sugar

Grease a shallow medium-sized baking dish. Place the milk, rum and eggs in a large mixing bowl and beat with a wire whisk until smooth and frothy. Add the caster sugar a little at a time and beat till the sugar is dissolved. Add the flour, sift it a little at a time, mixing in the salt with the last spoonful. Pour half of the batter into the prepared dish and spread the cherries over the top, then pour the remaining batter over all the cherries. Bake until the pudding is firm in the centre and sprinkle with a little icing sugar. Serve hot.

Red Fruit Crumble

PREPARATION TIME: 15 minutes

COOKING TIME: 25 minutes with a further 15 minutes

OVEN: 190°C (375°F) Gas Mark 5 reduced to 180°C (350°F) Gas Mark 4 after 25 minutes

2 level teaspoons cornflour
75g (3oz) granulated sugar
300g (12oz) raspberries, hulled
3 medium-sized ripe pears, peeled, quartered, cored and sliced.
100g (4oz) plain flour
50g (2oz) margarine
50g (2oz) soft brown sugar
25g (1oz) cornflakes or bran, crushed
Custard or cream

In a large mixing bowl, mix the cornflour and granulated sugar with the raspberries. Grease a 1.1 litre (2 pint) ovenproof dish. Arrange the mixture alternately with the pears. Sieve into another bowl the flour and rub in the margarine. Crush the cornflakes or bran flakes and stir in with the soft brown sugar. Put all the mixture over the fruit and flatten, using the back of the spoon. Cook in a moderate oven, temperature 190°C

(375°F) Gas Mark 5 for 25 minutes, then reduce the temperature to 180°C (350°F) Gas mark 4 and cook for 15 minutes until crumble is golden. Serve hot with custard or cream.

Honey Plum Cobbler

PREPARATION TIME: 30 minutes

COOKING TIME: 15 minutes plus a further 30 minutes

OVEN: 200°C (400°F) Gas Mark 6

1 kg (2lb) ripe plums, halved and stoned
4-6 tablespoons clear honey
225g (8oz) self-raising flour
2 tablespoons sugar
50g (2oz) butter or margarine
5-6 tablespoons milk
1 egg, beaten
Cream

Place the plums in an ovenproof dish with the honey, cover with a sheet of foil. Cook in a preheated oven for 15 minutes, temperature 200°C (400°F) Gas Mark 6. While the plums are cooking mix the flour and sugar and rub in the

butter or margarine. Using a knife stir in the milk and egg so the mixture forms a soft dough. Lightly flour the work surface and roll out the dough. Cut with 5cm (2 inch) cutter to form cobblers. Remove the plums from the oven and cool. Arrange the cobblers round the top of the dish overlapping slightly. Brush the top of each one with a little milk and sprinkle with sugar. Cook until golden. Serve hot with cream.

Les Bourdaines
(Apples Baked in Pastry)

PREPARATION TIME: 30 minutes

COOKING TIME: 20-25 minutes

OVEN: 160°C (325°F) Gas Mark 3

370g (12oz) plain flour
Pinch of salt
150g (6oz) butter
1½ tablespoons caster sugar
5-7 tablespoons iced water
6 large dessert apples, peeled and cored
6 tablespoons plum jam
1 egg, beaten, to glaze
Cream

Sift the flour and salt into a bowl. Rub in the butter until the mixture is like fine breadcrumbs. Stir in the sugar. Mix in enough water to give a smooth pliable dough. Divide the dough into 6 pieces and roll out each square. Fill the centres of the apples with jam and place an apple on each pastry square. Brush the edges of the squares with water and wrap up the apples, sealing them well. Cut out some pastry leaves and decorate. Place on a baking sheet. Brush the pastry with beaten egg, bake in a moderate pre-heated oven. Bake until golden brown. Serve hot with cream.

Alma Pudding with Wine Sauce

125g (4oz) butter
2 tablespoons sugar
2 eggs
4 tablespoons plain flour
2 tablespoons orange marmalade
½ teaspoon bicarbonate of soda
75ml (2½ fl oz) milk

Wine Sauce
1 egg
150ml (¼ pint) sherry
1 tablespoon sugar

Beat butter and sugar until light. Add eggs and flour. Add the marmalade, bicarbonate of soda and milk. Place mixture in a pudding basin and cover with foil, tied in place with string. Place in a large pan, pour in hot water until it comes ¾ of the way up the basin. Bring water to the boil and steam for 1 hour. Remove and turn out into a serving plate and serve with wine sauce.

Wine Sauce
Combine ingredients. Place over a pan of boiling water. Whisk until light and frothy. Serve.

This page: Red Fruit Crumble (top left), Cherry Clafoutis (top right) and Honey Plum Cobbler (bottom).

Facing page: Treacle Tart (top left), Les Bourdaines (top right), Apple and Nut Tart (centre) and Alma Pudding (bottom).

Winter Desserts

Yorkshire Apple Tart

PREPARATION TIME: 30 minutes	plus chilling
COOKING TIME: 25 minutes	15 minutes
OVEN: 190°C (375°F) Gas Mark 5	

275g (10oz) shortcrust pastry
350g (12oz) cooking apples, peeled, cored and sliced
2 tablespoons sugar
1 tablespoon water
Little milk and sugar to glaze
100g (4oz) strong cheese, sliced
Whipped cream

Roll out the pastry and use two-thirds to line a 20cm (8 inch) flan ring. Fill the centre with the sliced apples, sprinkle with sugar and water. Seal the edges, cover the tart with the remaining pastry, and brush the top with a little milk and sprinkle with sugar. Place in a preheated moderately hot oven and bake for 20 to 25 minutes until the crust is firm and lightly browned. Leave to cool, then with care remove the crust with a sharp knife. Place the cheese on top of the apples. Replace the crust. Return to the oven and bake for 15 minutes until the cheese has melted. Serve hot with whipped cream. Serves 4 to 6.

Fruit Cobbler

PREPARATION TIME: 20 minutes
COOKING TIME: 20 minutes
OVEN: 220°C (450°F) Gas Mark 7

250g (9oz) self raising flour
125g (4oz) butter
175ml (¼ pint) milk
3 large cooking apples
370g (12oz) can raspberries, drained
50g (2oz) granulated sugar
Cream
50g (2oz) demerara sugar

Sieve flour into a mixing bowl. Rub in butter excluding 10g (½oz), and work into a soft dough by adding milk. Knead the dough and roll out onto a floured board. Cut out the scones. Place the scones on a baking sheet and bake at 220°C (450°F) Gas Mark 7, for 10-15 minutes. Peel the apples and slice them. Put the apples in a saucepan, and cook in a little water with granulated sugar until soft. Drain the apples and add the raspberries. Cut the scones and sandwich together with butter. Put a circle of scones round the edge of the apple and raspberry mixture. Put some cream in the circle left by the scones. Sprinkle with a little demerara sugar and grill until the sugar begins to caramelise. Serve at

Snowballs

PREPARATION TIME: 20 minutes	
COOKING TIME: 30 minutes then	3 minutes
OVEN: 190°C (375°F) Gas Mark 5	

6 medium cooking apples
75g (3oz) soft brown sugar
¾ teaspoon mixed spice
2 eggs
75g (3oz) caster sugar
Glacé cherries and angelica (optional)

Wash and core the apples. Mix together soft brown sugar and all the spices and fill the centre of the apples. Put the apples on a baking tray and bake. Whisk the egg white until it peaks and fold in the caster sugar. Coat the apples with meringue and then return to the oven for a few minutes. Decorate with glacé cherries and angelica if desired.

Apple Betty

PREPARATION TIME: 30 minutes
COOKING TIME: 30 minutes
OVEN: 180°C (350°F) Gas Mark 4

100g (4oz) butter
100g (4oz) fresh white breadcrumbs
100g (4oz) soft brown sugar
½ level teaspoon ground cinnamon
Grated rind and juice of 1 lemon
800g (2lb) cooking apples, peeled, cored and sliced
3 tablespoons water
Ice cream or cream

Melt the butter in a saucepan. Take the pan off the heat and mix in the breadcrumbs. In a bowl mix the sugar, cinnamon and grated lemon rind. Add the apple slices. Butter the pie dish 1.2 litre (2 pint) size. Sprinkle some of the crumbs in the dish, layer the apple slices with crumb mixture, ending with the crumb mixture on top. Squeeze the lemon juice and spoon the water over the pudding. Cover the pudding with buttered foil and bake until apples are cooked. The topping should be crisp and golden. Serve with ice cream or cream.

Rainbow Tart

PREPARATION TIME: 15 minutes
COOKING TIME: 35 minutes
OVEN: 109°C (375°F) Gas Mark 5

Pastry
225g (8oz) plain flour
Pinch of salt
50g (2oz) butter or margarine
50g (2oz) lard
About 3 tablespoons water

Filling
1½ tablespoons strawberry jam
1½ tablespoons blackberry jam
1½ tablespoons bilberry jam
1½ tablespoons lemon curd
1½ tablespoons orange marmalade
1½ tablespoons gooseberry purée
1½ tablespoons mincemeat
Custard

Pastry
Sift flour and salt into a bowl. Cut the butter/margarine and lard into pieces and work into the flour with fingers until it looks like breadcrumbs. Stir the water into mixture and mix into a dough. Roll out the pastry on a lightly floured surface. Line a 23cm (9 inch) pie plate, trim the edges and reserve for twists.

Filling
Mark the dough and fill in the sections with the jams, curd and mincemeat. Twist the excess dough into spirals and use it to separate the jam sections. Brush the ends

with water and press onto the edge to seal. Flute the edge of pastry case and bake. Remove from the oven and leave to cool for 10 minutes. Serve with pouring custard.

Apple Dumplings with Walnut Sauce

PREPARATION TIME: 30 minutes
COOKING TIME: 35 minutes
OVEN: 200°C (400°F) Gas Mark 6

Dumplings
525g (18oz) shortcrust pastry
6 large cooking apples, cored
9 tablespoons mincemeat
1 egg, lightly beaten

Walnut Sauce
75g (3oz) butter
75g (3oz) light brown sugar
2½ tablespoons double cream
75g (3oz) chopped walnuts

Divide the dough into 6 portions. Roll out each portion into a round large enough to wrap up one apple. Place the apple in the centre of the dough round and fill the cavity (left by removing the core) with mincemeat. Wrap the dough round the apple and moisten the edges with beaten egg. Press together to seal. Place the dumplings on a baking sheet and brush all over with beaten egg. Bake in preheated moderately hot oven for 35 minutes or until golden brown. Meanwhile make the sauce.

Walnut Sauce
Melt the butter in a saucepan and stir in all the sugar. When the sugar has dissolved, stir in the cream and walnuts. Heat gently. Serve the dumplings with the sauce; both should be hot.

Facing page: Fruit Cobbler (top), Apple Betty (centre) and Yorkshire Apple Tart (bottom).

Winter Fruits

PREPARATION TIME: 15 minutes plus 1 hour soaking

COOKING TIME: 40 minutes

OVEN: 190°C (375°F) Gas Mark 5

100g (4oz) seedless raisins
100g (4oz) currants
100g (4oz) sultanas
100g (4oz) chopped mixed peel
Finely grated rind and juice of an orange
6 thick slices of toast, crusts removed
About 50g (2oz) butter or margarine
100g (4oz) soft brown sugar
300ml (½ pint) milk
2 eggs, lightly beaten
¼ teaspoon ground cinnamon
Custard

Put all the dried fruit, peel, orange rind and juice into a bowl and mix well. Put half the fruit mixture in the bottom of a buttered baking dish. Spread the toast with the butter or margarine, then cut it into small squares. Cover the fruit with half the toast and sprinkle with 50g (2oz) of the soft brown sugar. Repeat the layers again. Mix together the milk, eggs and cinnamon and pour over the layered pudding. Leave the pudding to soak for one hour. Bake in a preheated oven until crisp on top. Serve with thin pouring custard.

Apricot Pudding

PREPARATION TIME: 25 minutes

COOKING TIME: 2 hours

Pastry
175g (6oz) flour
Pinch of salt
50g (2oz) caster sugar
75g (3oz) shredded suet
5 tablespoons milk

Filling
1 cooking apple
175g (6oz) dried apricots, soaked overnight in cold water
50g (2oz) seedless raisins
½ teaspoon ground mixed spice
3 tablespoons golden syrup
2-3 tablespoons demerara sugar, to finish
Custard or cream

Pastry
Sift the flour and salt into a bowl. Stir in the sugar and suet, add the milk gradually and knead lightly to form a firm dough. Wrap the dough in foil and chill in the fridge.

Filling
Peel and core the apples, then grate into a bowl. Drain the apricots and chop them very finely, then mix in with all the other ingredients for the filling. Roll out the dough on a lightly floured surface. Cut out a small circle large enough to fit the base of a well buttered 900ml (1½ pint) pudding basin. Put the dough in the basin. Layer with fruit and a circle of dough (4 layers of dough, 3 layers of filling). Cover the top of the pudding with a circle of buttered greaseproof paper. Cover the basin with foil tied with string. Put the pudding basin in a steamer or in a pan half-filled with boiling water. Cover with a lid and steam. Keep the water level up. Remove the foil and greaseproof disc and let the pudding stand for a few minutes. Turn out carefully on a warmed serving plate and sprinkle with demerara sugar. Serve hot with pouring custard or cream.

Rhubarb Tart

PREPARATION TIME: 30 minutes

COOKING TIME: 40 minutes, then another 25 minutes

OVEN: 180°C (350°F) Gas Mark 4

Filling
1kg (2lb) rhubarb, cut into 2.5cm (1 inch) pieces.
525g (1lb 3oz) sugar
100g (4oz) butter
3 eggs
2 tablespoons white wine
250g (9oz) flour
2 teaspoons baking powder

Topping
150ml (¼ pint) soured cream
1 teaspoon ground cinnamon
50g (2oz) ground almonds
Icing sugar

Put the rhubarb pieces into a bowl, sprinkle with sugar (reserve 125g [5oz]). Cover and allow the rhubarb to draw. Cream the butter and 75g (3oz) of the granulated sugar. Mix together until light and fluffy. Stir in one egg and the wine. Sift in the flour and baking powder. Stir into the other ingredients. Knead the ingredients together to make a smooth dough. Form into a ball, wrap with greaseproof paper and allow to rest for 30 minutes in the fridge. Grease a 25cm (10 inch) loose-based or spring-clip tin. Roll out pastry on a well floured surface. Line tin with pastry. Strain the rhubarb, arrange in pastry case and bake.

Topping
Beat the cream and remaining eggs together and stir in the remaining sugar, the cinnamon and ground almonds. Mix thoroughly until smooth. Take the tart out of the oven and pour the topping over the rhubarb. Return to the oven and bake for another 25 minutes. Remove from the oven, turn out and dust with icing sugar, cool before serving.

Facing page: Rhubarb Tart (top), Winter Fruits (bottom left) and Apricot Pudding (bottom right).

Carrot Pudding

PREPARATION TIME: 15 minutes

COOKING TIME: 45 minutes

OVEN: 180°C (350°F) Gas Mark 4

50g (2oz) butter or margarine
50g (2oz) sugar
2 eggs, separated
50g (2oz) plain flour
1 teaspoon ground cinnamon
225g (8oz) carrots, peeled and grated
1 tablespoon chopped walnuts
4 tablespoons dry red wine
Grated rind, and juice of 1 lemon
Pinch of salt

Cream the butter or margarine with the sugar until the mixture is light and fluffy. Beat in the egg yolks. Sift in the flour and cinnamon, carrots, walnuts, wine, lemon rind, juice and salt. Beat the egg whites until stiff and fold into carrot mixture. Pour into a greased baking dish. Bake in a preheated moderate oven. Serve hot from the dish.

Orange Round

PREPARATION TIME: 30 minutes

COOKING TIME: 15 minutes for pastry 20 minutes for filled flan

OVEN: 180°C (350°F) Gas Mark 4

318g (10oz) shortcrust pastry
3 oranges, thinly sliced
2 eggs, beaten
75g (3oz) ground almonds
3 tablespoons sugar
3 tablespoons clear honey

Roll out the pastry and line a 20cm (8 inch) flan dish. Prick the base of the flan. Cut a piece of greaseproof paper, line the pastry and sprinkle with baking beans (or any dried beans, to bake blind). Bake for 10 minutes at 190°C (375°F) Gas Mark 5. While the case is baking, prepare the orange filling. Put the oranges in a saucepan. Add enough water to cover the oranges and simmer for 20 minutes. Cook until the orange peel is soft and drain

the water. Beat the egg, almonds and sugar until smooth. Spread the mixture in the flan case. Arrange the poached orange slices on top of the mixture. Spoon the clear honey over all the slices. Cook the flan for 20 minutes.

Yuletide Pudding (Round)

PREPARATION TIME: 30 minutes

COOKING TIME: 5 hours plus 3 hours before serving

350g (12oz) mixed dried fruit
150g (6oz) stoned raisins
75g (3oz) chopped mixed peel
350g (12oz) soft dark brown sugar
40g (1½oz) almonds, blanched and chopped
150g (6oz) fresh white breadcrumbs
150g (6oz) shredded suet
150g (6oz) plain flour
½ level teaspoon ground nutmeg
½ level teaspoon ground cinnamon
¼ level teaspoon salt
1 carrot, grated
1 cooking apple, peeled, cored and grated
Grated rind and juice of 1 lemon
3 tablespoons brandy
1 large egg

Put all ingredients in a large mixing bowl and blend together well. Grease 2 1.2 litre (2 pint) pudding basins. Put the mixture into the pudding basins, dividing the

mixture evenly between both. Fill the basins, but leave a gap of about 2.5cm (1 inch) at the top. Cover both puddings with buttered round of greaseproof paper. Make a foil pudding lid with a pleat and tie securely onto basin. Stand the puddings in pans and add enough water to keep the pans two-thirds full. Cover the pans and boil for 5 hours. Keep the pans topped up with hot water. Remove the basins from water and gently loosen one pudding from its basin, turn it out onto the other pudding. Press the puddings together to make one pudding. Press down on the top pudding. Leave to cool completely, then cover together with greaseproof paper and foil. Before serving boil for three hours. Again make sure the water is topped up. Unwrap carefully and turn out of the bowl.

Pacific Pudding

225g (8oz) can pineapple rings
100g (4oz) caster sugar
100g (4oz) soft margarine
Grated rind of 1 orange
2 eggs, beaten
75g (3oz) self raising flour, sifted
50g (2oz) white breadcrumbs
50g (2oz) glacé cherries, quartered
50g (2oz) stoned raisins
25g (1oz) angelica
2 tablespoons golden syrup

Drain the pineapple and keep the juice. Cut 3 rings in half and reserve. Chop the remainder coarsely. Cream together the margarine and sugar, add the orange rind and beat in the eggs. Fold in the flour and breadcrumbs. Add the chopped pineapple, cherries, raisins and angelica, and mix well. Butter a 900ml (1½ pint) pudding basin. Put the syrup in the bottom and arrange the pineapple rings in a circle. Spoon in the sponge mixture on top and level it. Cover with buttered paper and foil. Put the pudding basin in a saucepan of boiling water two-thirds full. Boil for 1¾ hours. Serve with tangy butter.

This page: Rainbow Tart (top), Carrot Pudding (centre) and Apple Dumplings with Walnut Sauce (bottom).

Facing page: Yuletide Pudding (top), Pacific Pudding (centre left), Orange Round (centre right) and Snowball (bottom).

Special Desserts

Ginger Rum Trifle

PREPARATION TIME: 20 minutes

1½ cups ginger cake, sliced
1½ cups canned pear quarters
9 tablespoons rum
1¾ cups cold thick vanilla sauce
1¼ cups heavy cream
2-3 teaspoons confectioners' sugar
Toasted flaked almonds
Stem ginger cut into strips

Line the bottom of a glass dish with half the ginger cake. Drain the canned pears and mix the rum with the juice. Sprinkle half over the cake. Place the pears on the top of the cake and cover with the remaining slices. Pour over a little more rum mixture. Spoon the sauce over the cake. Whip the cream and gradually add confectioners' sugar until it peaks. Spoon the cream over the sauce and decorate with lightly toasted almond flakes and stem ginger strips.

Lemon Brandy Cream

PREPARATION TIME: 15 minutes

1¼ cups light cream
1¼ cups heavy cream
6 tablespoons soft brown sugar
2 large lemons
6 tablespoons sponge cake
2 tablespoons brandy
2 tablespoons toasted flaked almonds

Mix the light and heavy cream in a small saucepan and add the sugar. Stir over a low heat until the cream begins to bubble. Grate the rind of the lemons and gently stir into the cream. Leave the mixture to cool and crumble the cake crumbs into glasses or serving dish. Stir the brandy into the cream mixture with the juice from both lemons. Pour the mixture into the glasses or dish over the cake crumbs and refrigerate for 30 minutes. Decorate with toasted almond flakes.

Exotic Fruit Salad Basket

PREPARATION TIME: 15 minutes

1 large melon
1 persimmon
3 kiwi fruit, washed
4oz blackberries, washed
6oz raspberries, washed
6oz redcurrants, washed
6oz strawberries, washed
6oz blackcurrants, washed
6oz grapes, red and green

1 mango, peeled and sliced
Strawberry leaves
Use as many fruits in season as are available
Sugar syrup (see Sauces)

Hollow out a melon and reserve the pulp. Slice the persimmon and kiwi fruit, and make melon balls using the reserved melon. Arrange the fruit in the melon basket and spoon over with sugar syrup (see Sauces).

Cranberry Fool, Chilled

PREPARATION TIME: 30 minutes

450g (1lb) cranberries
125g (5oz) sugar
2 tablespoons lemon juice
150ml (5 fl oz) carton soured cream

Bring the cranberries to the boil in 450ml (¾ pint) water in a saucepan, then simmer for about 15 minutes. Cool and stir in the sugar until dissolved. Purée the mixture until most of it is smooth by rubbing it through a sieve to remove the cranberry skins. Make sure the mixture is cool, stir in the lemon juice, cover and chill. Spoon into serving dish and serve with sour cream.

Berry Whip

PREPARATION TIME: 15 minutes

3 egg whites
A few grains of salt
150g (6oz) icing sugar
200g (8oz) blackberries
Sponge fingers

In a deep bowl whisk the egg whites. Add the sugar and salt and beat until very stiff. Fold in the berries. Spoon into glasses and chill. Serve with sponge fingers.

Cremets

PREPARATION TIME: 10 minutes

300g (12oz) curd cheese
25g (1oz) vanilla sugar or caster sugar with a few drops of vanilla essence
300ml (½ pint) double cream

Beat the curd cheese until smooth. Add the sugar and gradually beat in the cream. Pile into a bowl and chill.

Almond Galette

PREPARATION TIME: 1 hour
COOKING TIME: 10 minutes for each batch of rounds
OVEN: 190°C (375°F) Gas Mark 5

350g (12oz) butter
450g (1lb) caster sugar
2 eggs
300g (11oz) plain flour
2 tablespoons ground almonds
900ml (1½ pints) double or whipping cream, whipped
Icing sugar
Double cream
Whole almonds

Cut out 12 22cm (9 inch) circles of non-stick baking paper. Cream the sugar and butter together and beat in the eggs. Fold in the sifted flour and ground almonds. Divide the mixture into 12 and using a large palette knife coat the individual paper rounds with the mixture. Work from the centre outwards with smooth strokes. Wet a baking sheet and bake the rounds. Leave until cool and carefully peel off the paper. When all the rounds are cooked use them to form layers spreading each one with whipped

cream. Reserve 150ml (5 fl oz) of cream for decoration. Dust the top with icing sugar and decorate with almonds and cream.

Blackberry, Raisin and Walnut Jelly

PREPARATION TIME: 10 minutes
Note: In order that the fruit should be plump, soak overnight.

100g (4oz) seedless raisins
2 tablespoons rum
1 packet blackberry jelly
300ml (½ pint) port
400g (1lb) frozen blackberries (keep frozen)
6 walnuts halved
Cream
Flowers

Soak the raisins in the rum for a few hours, preferably overnight. Dissolve the jelly in 300ml (½ pint) of boiling water. Add the port and cool, making sure the jelly does not set. Put the fruit and nuts in individual glasses or a mould making sure they are quite full. Spoon over the jelly and leave to set. Decorate with flowers and/or cream.

French Plum Pudding

PREPARATION TIME: 20 minutes
COOKING TIME: 40 minutes
OVEN: 200°C (400°F) Gas Mark 6

175g (6oz) plain flour
175g (6oz) butter
75g (3oz) caster sugar
50g (2oz) ground almonds
1 egg yolk
1 tablespoon cold water
750g (1½lb) plums, halved and stoned

Sift the flour into a mixing bowl. Rub in two-thirds of the butter and 25g (1oz) of the sugar. Add the ground almonds and mix into a firm dough with the egg yolk and water. Chill. Melt the reserved butter in a 23cm (9 inch) round ovenproof dish. Add the remaining sugar until caramelised. Remove from heat. Arrange the plums, skin side down, in the ovenproof dish. On a lightly floured surface roll out the dough into a round slightly bigger than the dish. Place the dough on top of the plums and gently press down, tucking in the edges as you go. Bake in the oven until golden. To serve turn out onto a serving dish. Serve instantly.

Chocolate Meringues

PREPARATION TIME: 40 minutes
COOKING TIME: 2 hours
(leave the meringues to cool for as long as necessary)
OVEN: 120°C (250°F) Gas Mark ½

4 egg whites
225g (8oz) caster sugar
50g (2oz) hazelnuts, finely ground
300ml (10 fl oz) double or whipping cream
1 tablespoon cocoa powder
Chocolate curls

Whisk the egg whites until stiff. Gently whisk in the sugar a little at a time and fold in the hazelnuts with a metal spoon. Spoon out rounds of meringue onto a baking sheet lined with non-stick silicone paper or lightly oiled greaseproof paper. Bake until well dried out. Cool on wire racks. Whip the cream until stiff and fold in the cocoa powder. Use the cream to sandwich the meringues and decorate with chocolate shavings or curls.

Coconut Cup

PREPARATION TIME: 35 minutes

3 coconuts sawed in half
3 scoops soft-scoop vanilla ice cream per half coconut
3 tablespoons dark rum
450g (1lb) dried mixed fruit

Soak fruit in rum overnight. Saw coconuts in half and remove the flesh. Grate half the flesh, and incorporate in the ice cream along with the fruit, reserving some of the fruit for decoration. Fill coconut halves with mixture and place in freezer until firm. To serve, top with remaining fruit and grated coconut.

This page: Cremet (left), Almond Galette (right).

Facing page: Blackberry, Raisin and Walnut Jelly (top right), French Plum Pudding (centre left) and Chocolate Meringues (bottom).

Blackberry Ice Cream Dessert

PREPARATION TIME: 20 minutes plus freezing time

75g (3oz) sugar
1½ tablespoons Curaçao
300g (11oz) blackberry purée
175ml (6 fl oz) low-fat plain yogurt
Generous pinch of cinnamon
150ml (¼ pint) double or whipping cream, whipped
150ml (5 fl oz) water

Boil the sugar with the water for a minute and add the Curaçao. Stir in the blackberry purée (rub the fruit through a nylon sieve). Stir in the yogurt and cinnamon, and lastly fold in the whipped cream. Freeze until creamy and serve.

Kiwi Cheesecake

PREPARATION TIME: 45 minutes
COOKING TIME: 20 minutes
OVEN: 180°C (350°F) Gas Mark 4

Base
50g (2oz) soft margarine
50g (2oz) caster sugar
1 egg
65g (2½oz) self raising flour
½ level teaspoon baking powder
Finely grated rind of ½ medium orange

Filling
150g (6oz) cream cheese
50g (2oz) caster sugar
3 eggs, separated
Juice of 1 medium orange
Finely grated rind of ½ medium orange
15g (½oz) gelatine
4 tablespoons cold water
125g (5oz) natural yogurt
150ml (¼ pint) whipping cream

To decorate
150ml (¼ pint) whipped cream
3 kiwi fruit, peeled and sliced
Nuts

Base
Grease and line the base and sides of a 20cm (8 inch) loose bottom cake tin with greaseproof paper. Note: The paper should come over the top of the tin. In a mixing bowl add the margarine, egg and caster sugar and cream the mixture until fluffy. Sieve the flour and baking

powder into the bowl and beat. Add the orange rind. Use either a wooden spoon or electric whisk for two or one minute respectively. Spoon the mixture into the cake tin and cook for 20 minutes, 180°C (350°F) Gas Mark 4. Leave in tin when cooked and allow to cool.

Filling
While the base is cooking, beat the sugar with cream cheese and add the egg yolks, orange juice and rind. Beat until very smooth. In a heatproof basin put the cold water and sprinkle in the gelatine, leaving it to stand for 10 minutes until soft. Stand the basin in a pan of simmering water until gelatine dissolves. Stir constantly. Leave to cool but not set. Pour the gelatine in a constant stream into the cheese mixture and stir. Whisk in the yogurt. Whip the cream and fold carefully into the mixture using a metal spoon. Whisk the egg whites in a clean bowl until stiff

and fold into cheese mixture. Pour the cheese mixture over the base and smooth the top. Leave to set in the fridge for several hours.

To decorate
Remove from the tin and carefully peel off the paper, serve decorated with cream, kiwi fruit and nuts (an alternative could be orange segments). Serve chilled.

Poached Minty Pears

PREPARATION TIME: 40 minutes plus chilling

6 large pears, peeled
6 tablespoons sugar
Fresh mint leaves
6 tablespoons clear honey
3 tablespoons Creme de Menthe liqueur

Put the pears in a saucepan. Stand upright and pour water over. Cover all the pears. Boil and then simmer for 30 minutes. Pour off half the water and sprinkle over with sugar. Add the fresh mint and simmer for 10 minutes. Transfer the pears to a bowl. Reserve 150ml (¼ pint) water from the pan and stir in the honey and liqueur. Pour this mixture over the pears and allow it to cool. Cover the pears and chill for 2 hours. Stand each pear on an individual serving dish and spoon over the mint sauce.

This page: Blackberry Ice Cream Dessert (top), Coconut Cups (bottom).

Facing page: Kiwi Cheesecake (top), Poached Minty Pear (bottom).

Coffee Truffles

PREPARATION TIME: 10 minutes

200-225g (8oz) cake crumbs
25g (1oz) ground almonds
¼ teaspoon coffee powder
Heaped tablespoon apricot jam,
    melted
2-3 tablespoons coffee liqueur
50g (2oz) chocolate vermicelli

Put the crumbs and ground almonds into a bowl. Mix in the jam and coffee liqueur and mix together to form a stiff paste. Shape into small balls and roll in chocolate vermicelli.

Crystal Fruits

1 egg white
200g (8oz) bunch of grapes
2 large red apples
2 large pears
100g (4oz) plums
Any other soft fruit in season

Whisk up the egg white well and brush onto the fruit. Leave for a few minutes but not until dry. Dip the fruit into caster sugar and place on greaseproof paper until dry. Arrange in fruit bowl or stand.

Apricot Mountain

PREPARATION TIME: 20 minutes

COOKING TIME: 4 minutes or until meringue is brown

OVEN: 230°C (450°F) Gas Mark 8

About 350g (¾lb) tinned apricot
    halves
4-6 tablespoons Marsala or sweet
    sherry
3 egg whites
100g (4oz) caster sugar
1 x 20cm (8 inch) sponge flan case
450ml (¾ pint) vanilla ice cream

Strain the apricots and sprinkle them with the sherry. Whisk the egg whites until stiff and fold in the sugar. Whisk again until the meringue peaks. Stand the flan case on a heatproof dish and sprinkle with a little more sherry. Pile the apricots into the flan case. Cover the apricots with a mountain shape of ice cream. Using the meringue mixture, quickly cover the ice cream and the sponge base. Bake immediately until the meringue is light brown. Serve from the oven. For a very special effect bury half an egg shell at the top of the mountain before baking the meringue. As you serve fill it with warmed brandy, ignite and serve flaming.

Petits Fours

PREPARATION TIME: 40 minutes

OVEN: 200°C (400°F) Gas Mark 6

Sponge
3 eggs
125g (4oz) caster sugar
75g (3oz) plain flour
1 tablespoon hot water

Topping
Fruits in season
Apricot jam to glaze

Sponge
Whisk eggs and sugar until thick and creamy. Sift in flour and fold in with the hot water. Place mixture in a greased and floured swiss roll tin. Bake for 8 to 10 minutes until cake springs back when pressed. Turn out and cool. Cut shapes out of the sponge using pastry cutters.

Topping
Place sponge shapes on a wire rack and top with attractively arranged fruit. Melt apricot jam on low heat and spoon over shapes to glaze. When surplus has dripped off and jam has set remove and place on serving plate.

Chocolate Leaf, Filled with Orange Mousse

PREPARATION TIME: 1 hour
                    plus chilling

For the Leaf
175g (6oz) plain chocolate
1 cabbage leaf (with veins)

Mousse
3 whole eggs plus 2 yolks
50g (2oz) caster sugar
Juice of ½ lemon
15g (½oz) powdered gelatine
150ml (¼ pint) double cream
150ml (¼ pint) freshly squeezed
    orange juice
Finely grated rind of 2 oranges

Leaf
Put the chocolate in a basin over simmering water and stir until smooth. With a pastry brush, paint the chocolate over a well-veined cabbage leaf and leave to cool and harden. Repeat the process until there is a thick build up of chocolate on the leaf. When hard the cabbage leaf can be easily removed.

Mousse
Put the eggs and yolks in a basin with the caster sugar. Whisk until pale and frothy. This can be done over a saucepan of simmering water, but make sure that the basin doesn't touch the water. Beat until thick. Remove from the heat and whisk until cold. Put the lemon juice and a little water into a small saucepan and sprinkle in the gelatine and leave it to soak for a few minutes. Whip the cream and stir it into the egg mixture, gradually adding the orange juice and grated rind. Gently heat the gelatine until clear and stir it quickly into the mixture. Fill the serving dish and refrigerate until set. This mousse can either be served with one leaf or several small leaves to go with each portion of mousse.

Crystal Fruits (left), Coffee Truffles (bottom left) and Petits Fours (bottom right).

Fruit Salad with Mango Purée

PREPARATION TIME: 20 minutes plus 1 hour chilling in the refrigerator

3 peaches
3 tamarillos (tree tomatoes)
3 kiwi fruit
1½ tablespoons lemon juice
3 tablespoons sugar syrup

Mango Purée
2 well-ripened mangoes weighing about 300g (12oz)
Juice of ½ a lime, or lemon
3 teaspoons honey
125g (5oz) redcurrants
Strawberry leaves for decoration

Blanch the peaches briefly and peel. Halve and remove stones and cut into delicate wedges. Peel and slice the tamarillos, nectarines and kiwi fruit, arrange in serving dish and scatter over with redcurrants. Pour over the lemon juice mixed with sugar syrup. Leave the fruits to stand in syrup for 1 hour in a cool place.

Mango Purée
Either liquidise or rub through a wire sieve the flesh of the mangoes and mix with the lime juice. Mix in the honey and pour the mixture over the fruit. Decorate with strawberry leaves.

Pineapple Malibu

PREPARATION TIME: 30 minutes

1 medium ripe pineapple
450ml (15 fl oz) double cream
75g (3oz) macaroons, roughly crushed
3 tablespoons coconut liqueur

Cut the pineapple a few inches below the top. Scoop out as much of the fruit as possible, discarding the core if hard. Chop the fruit into bite-size pieces. Whip two-thirds of the cream until it begins to stiffen and fold in the macaroons, having first soaked them in the coconut liqueur. In another bowl whip up the remaining cream and fold into the coconut cream. Spoon alternate spoonfuls of diced pineapple and cream mixture into the hollowed pineapple and chill. Serve straight from the fridge.

Chocolate Ginger Flan

PREPARATION TIME: 30 minutes

100g (4oz) plain chocolate
300ml (½ pint) milk
100g (4oz) caster sugar
3 tablespoons flour
100g (4oz) butter
2 egg yolks
150g (6oz) ginger nut biscuits
Whipped cream
100g (4oz) stem ginger cut into thin slices

Melt the chocolate in the milk in a saucepan, stirring constantly.

Remove pan from heat. Mix the caster sugar, flour and 50g (2oz) butter into the chocolate milk and stir in the egg yolks. Put on a low heat and slowly bring to the boil. Simmer for 5 minutes until the mixture begins to thicken, stir until smooth. Remove from heat and cool. While the filling is cooling, melt the remaining 50g (2oz) of butter and crush the ginger nut biscuits. Mix the biscuits with the melted butter and press in a greased pie mould. When the filling is cool, pour onto the ginger nut base. Chill and decorate with whipped cream and sprinkle with stemmed ginger cut into thin slices

(an alternative decoration is chocolate vermicelli).

Coffee Charlotte

PREPARATION TIME: 1½ hours
COOKING TIME: 12 minutes
OVEN: 220°C (475°F) Gas Mark 7

Sponge
4 egg yolks
50g (2oz) sugar
Generous pinch of salt
3 egg whites
60g (2½oz) flour mixed with 2 teaspoons coffee powder

tablespoon of brandy. Add to the custard mixture and stir well. Cool the custard. Meanwhile stiffly whip the cream, adding the remaining sugar. When the custard begins to set, carefully fold in the cream and fill the sponge-lined mould. Stir in the marinated apricot and cover the top of the mould with slices from the sponge roll. Let the charlotte set for three hours in the refrigerator and turn onto a serving dish. Brush with the apricot glaze.

Orange Campari Mousse

PREPARATION TIME: 45 minutes
plus chilling

1 teaspoon powdered gelatine
2 medium oranges, washed and dried
75g (3oz) caster sugar
2 eggs, separated
3 tablespoons Campari
150ml (¼ pint) double cream
1 tablespoon cold milk
Red grapes

Add gelatine to two tablespoons of water in a saucepan. Leave to one side. Grate peel of 1 orange. Squeeze oranges and if necessary make up juice to 175ml (6 fl oz) with water. Melt gelatine and water over a low heat. Stir in orange juice. Pour mixture into a bowl, whisk in sugar, egg yolks, Campari and orange peel. Place in fridge until the mixture begins to thicken and set. In one bowl beat egg whites until stiff. In another whisk milk and cream together thick. Gradually mix egg whites and cream alternately into the orange mixture until totally incorporated. Pour into a bowl and place in refrigerator until firm and set. Serve in glasses decorated with sliced red grapes.

175g (6oz) apricot jam
3 tablespoons brandy
2 tablespoons cornflour

Charlotte
6 apricot halves
1 tablespoon vanilla sugar
1 tablespoon brandy
4 egg yolks
100g (4oz) sugar
Plus 1 tablespoon sugar
250ml (8 fl oz) milk
½ vanilla pod
15g (½oz) powdered gelatine
250ml (8 fl oz) double or whipping cream
75ml (2½ fl oz) apricot glaze (warmed apricot jam)

Sponge
Beat the egg yolks with a spoonful of sugar and the salt. Whisk the egg whites and fold the egg yolk mixture into the meringue. Sift together the cornflour and flour and stir them in. Line a swiss roll tin with non-stick silicone paper or greaseproof paper. Spread the sponge mixture evenly in the swiss roll tin using a spatula. Bake until golden. Turn it out at once onto a damp tea towel and peel off the paper. Blend the jam with the brandy and spread the sponge cake with it. Roll it up. Let it cool and cut into thin slices 5mm (¼ inch) thick. Line the mould with the

slices as close together as possible.

Charlotte
Place the apricot halves in a dish and sprinkle them with vanilla sugar. Pour over the brandy. Leave them to marinate in the refrigerator for half an hour. Cream the egg yolks and sugar together in a mixing bowl and put the milk in a small saucepan with the vanilla pod. Heat the milk and bring to the boil and pour into the egg yolks. Return the custard mixture to the saucepan and stir until it is thick enough to coat the spoon. Remove from heat. Dissolve the gelatine in warm water and stir in the

Facing page: Apricot Mountain (left), Orange Campari Mousse (right).

This page: Chocolate Leaf, Filled with Orange Mousse (top), Chocolate Ginger Flan (centre left) and Fruit Salad with Mango Purée (bottom right).

Chestnut Parfait

PREPARATION TIME: 40 minutes
plus freezing

4 egg yolks
150g (5oz) sugar
150ml (¼ pint) milk, warmed and
    flavoured with a vanilla pod
200g (7oz) unsweetened chestnut
    purée
2 tablespoons dark rum
2 egg whites
50g (2oz) sugar
500ml (17 fl oz) double cream
Chocolate leaves
A few cranberries
Whipped cream

Beat the egg yolks with the sugar and add the warmed milk flavoured with the vanilla pod and cook until thickened, stirring gently. The mixture should coat the spoon. Transfer to a mixing bowl. Add the chestnut purée and rum while the mixture is still lukewarm. Chill well. Whip the egg whites with the sugar until very stiff. Whisk the cream until it peaks. Fold the egg white into the chestnut custard and carefully fold in the whipped cream. Pour into a 1.5 litre (2¾ pint) mould and freeze for 4 hours. Decorate with small rounds of sweetened chestnut purée dusted with chocolate powder or melted chocolate sauce.

Strawberry Shortcake

PREPARATION TIME: 1 hour
COOKING TIME: 25 minutes
OVEN: 220°C (425°F) Gas Mark 7

Shortcake

225g (8oz) plain flour
Pinch of salt
4 teaspoons baking powder
75g (3oz) butter
1 large egg
40g (1½oz) caster sugar
3 tablespoons milk
1 tablespoon melted butter

Filling

1 tablespoon custard powder
300ml (½ pint) milk
2 tablespoons sugar
150ml (¼ pint) double cream
450g (1lb) fresh or thawed, frozen
    strawberries
8 toasted almonds

Shortcake

Sift the flour, salt and baking powder into a bowl. With a knife mix in the butter. Beat in the egg, sugar and milk and pour into the centre of the dry ingredients. Mix into a dough. On a lightly floured surface knead gently and divide into two. Brush a 20cm (8 inch) sandwich tin with melted butter and shape half the dough into a circle to fit. Place the second circle on top and bake until risen and golden brown. Cool and separate the two halves.

Filling

Make up the custard using the milk and sugar. Cover and leave to cool. Whisk the cream until just stiff. Fold the cream into the cooled custard, reserving two tablespoons for decoration. Reserving 8 whole strawberries and one-third of the custard mixture, halve the remaining strawberries and mix into the custard cream. Spread the strawberry custard on the bottom layer of the shortbread and sandwich with the top layer. Spread the top with the reserved custard mixture and decorate with whole strawberries and almonds.

Green Devils

PREPARATION TIME: 20 minutes
plus chilling

600g (1½lb) dessert gooseberries
150g (6oz) caster sugar
600ml (1 pint) water
3 tablespoons grenadine
Juice ½ lemon
1 level tablespoon cornflour
Cream

Rinse and top and tail the gooseberries. Put the caster sugar in a small saucepan and dissolve it in the water. Simmer and bring to the boil. Take off heat and stir in the grenadine, lemon juice and gooseberries and bring back to simmer. Cook very gently for five minutes until the fruit is tender. Remove from heat. Lift out the fruit and put into the serving dish. Mix the cornflour with a little water to make a thin paste. Stir into the fruit juice till it begins to thicken. Stir all the time. When the syrup is clear, pour over the fruit. Chill, preferably overnight, and serve with thick pouring cream.

Facing page: Pineapple Malibu (top), Coffee Charlotte (centre right) and Chestnut Parfait (bottom).

This page: Green Devils (top), Strawberry Shortcake (bottom).

Quick Desserts

Zabaglione

PREPARATION TIME: 5 minutes

COOKING TIME: 10 minutes

4 egg yolks
4 tablespoons caster sugar
4 tablespoons Marsala wine

Put all the ingredients into a large heatproof bowl. Beat with a balloon whisk until light and frothy. Stand the bowl in a pan of water over a low heat and continue to whisk. The mixture will froth and is now ready to serve. Pour into heatproof glasses and serve immediately with the sponge fingers. An instant Italian dessert. Note: Do not overheat or the mixture will curdle and not become frothy.

Raspberry Brioches

PREPARATION TIME: 15 minutes

12 small brioches (use either fresh or frozen brioches, or choux buns as illustrated).
50g (2oz) sugar
1 tablespoon lemon juice
2 tablespoons honey
Scant 150ml (¼ pint) water
1 teaspoon raspberry liqueur
400g (1lb) fresh raspberries
2 tablespoons toasted, flaked almonds

Let the sugar, lemon juice, honey and water boil for three minutes. Add the raspberry liqueur. Using some of the syrup, soak the brioches. Fill with the raspberries. Sprinkle over the rest of the syrup and add the flaked almonds. Serve.

This page: Poor Knights of Windsor (top left), Zabaglione (top right) and Coffee Liqueur Crêpes (bottom).

Facing page: Lemon Syllabub (top), Hot Fruit Brioches (centre) and Raspberry Brioches (bottom).

Hot Fruit Brioches

PREPARATION TIME: 20 minutes

12 small brioches
75g (3oz) sugar
Scant 150ml (¼pint) water
300g (10oz) apricots, peeled and
*   halved*
150g (6oz) fresh blackberries
3 tablespoons brandy

Sabayon Sauce
6 egg yolks
200g (7oz) sugar
250ml (8 fl oz) very dry white wine

Heat the sugar and water in a saucepan. Add the apricots and poach until glossy. Meanwhile make up the sabayon sauce and reserve. Add the blackberries and brandy, leave for 4 minutes and reserve them. Cut the tops off the brioches and hollow them. Fill the hollowed brioches with the poached apricots and saturate the top with remaining syrup. Pour over sabayon sauce and put the lid on.

Sabayon Sauce
Cream the egg yolks and sugar together. Place the bowl over warm water and add the wine. Stir continuously. A last minute alternative. They are delicious with hot stewed fruit, and the sabayon sauce adds a dash of extravagance.

Poor Knights of Windsor

PREPARATION TIME and COOKING TIME: 15 minutes inclusive

1 egg
1 tablespoon of milk
2 tablespoons caster sugar
6 small slices of fruit or plain bread,
*   crusts removed*
50g (2oz) butter
1 teaspoon ground cinnamon

To decorate
350g (15oz) can apricot halves in
*   juice (drained)*
Whipped cream
1 tablespoon toasted almonds

Beat the egg and mix with sugar and milk. Dip the bread into the custard mixture and fry. Sprinkle bread with ground cinnamon and decorate with apricot halves, whipped cream and toasted almonds. Serve hot.

Coffee Liqueur Crêpes

PREPARATION TIME: 35 minutes

Crêpes
100g (4oz) plain flour
Pinch of salt
1 teaspoon caster sugar
250ml (8 fl oz) cold milk
1 egg
4 tablespoons cold strong black coffee
1 teaspoon vegetable oil
Oil for frying

Sauce
15g (½oz) butter
Grated rind and juice of ½ a lemon
2 tablespoons coffee liqueur

Crêpes
Sift the flour, salt and sugar into a bowl. Add the milk, egg, coffee and oil and whisk until smooth. Lightly oil a frying pan and fry the crêpes until golden brown. Toss and cook on the other side. Keep the crêpes warm.

Sauce
Melt the butter in a large frying pan. Arrange the crêpes folded in the pan. Add the lemon rind and juice and coffee liqueur. Heat gently until hot. Serve immediately.

Syllabub

PREPARATION TIME: 10 minutes plus overnight soaking

Thinly pared rind of 1 lemon
6 tablespoons of lemon juice
9 tablespoons sweet white wine or
*   sherry*
15ml (3 tablespoons) brandy
75g (3oz) caster sugar
450ml (¾ pint) double cream
Grated nutmeg

Put the lemon rind and juice, brandy and wine or sherry in a bowl. Leave overnight. Remove the lemon rind and stir in the sugar. Gradually stir in the cream until it peaks. This will require beating. Spoon into glasses and sprinkle with grated nutmeg.

Caramel Oranges

PREPARATION TIME: 15 minutes

6 oranges (large and juicy)
150g (6oz) caster sugar
450ml (¾ pint) water

Peel the oranges. Put the sugar and water in a heavy saucepan. Boil the mixture until it begins to caramelise. Place the oranges in a presentation dish and pour over the liquid caramel. Serve immediately.

Blackberry Fluff

PREPARATION TIME: 10 minutes

450g (1lb) blackberries, drained
300ml (10 fl oz) double cream
1 egg white
50g (2oz) caster sugar
Pieces of angelica to decorate
Sponge finger biscuits

Sieve the blackberries. Whip the cream until thick and stir into the blackberry purée. Beat the egg white, adding the sugar slowly until the mixture is stiff. Fold the egg white into the blackberry cream. Spoon into individual serving glasses and serve with sponge finger biscuits. A quick and luscious dessert. Make it in advance but in individual glasses. Store in the refrigerator and serve chilled.

Spiced Pears

PREPARATION TIME: 20 minutes

750g (1½lb) can of pear halves
450ml (¾pint) red wine
3 teaspoons ground cinnamon
75g (3oz) stem ginger, chopped

Drain the pears, saving 150ml (¼ pint) of the juice. Put the pears in the wine, with the juice and cinnamon. Boil for 10 minutes and reduce the heat. Simmer for ten minutes. Add the chopped ginger and leave to cool. Serve chilled.

Cherries Jubilee

PREPARATION TIME: 10 minutes

375g (1½lb) tinned black cherries
1½ tablespoons grated lemon rind
75g (3 tablespoons) cornflour
6 tablespoons brandy
Vanilla ice cream

Drain the cherries, reserving the tinned juice. Put all except one tablespoon of juice into a saucepan, add the lemon rind and bring to the boil. Simmer for 2 minutes and strain the juice. Return the juice to the saucepan and add the cherries. In the reserved tablespoon of juice, dissolve the cornflour. Add this to the saucepan and stir constantly until thick. Warm the brandy and set it alight. Pour it as it flames into the cherry mixture and stir until the flames die down. Serve immediately with ice cream.

Redcurrant and Blackcurrant Compote

PREPARATION TIME: 10 minutes plus chilling

750g (1½lb) redcurrants (or 350g
*   (12oz) each of redcurrants and*
*   blackcurrants)*
275g (10oz) sugar
1 tablespoon water
2 tablespoons gin or brandy
Whipped cream
Sponge finger biscuits

Put the fruit, sugar and water into a saucepan. Shake gently over the heat until sugar has dissolved. Remove from heat and stir in the gin or brandy. Cool. Spoon the compote into serving dishes. Chill for three hours before serving. Serve in the cream and sponge finger biscuits.

Tarte Aux Fruits

PREPARATION TIME: 15 minutes

1 pastry or sponge flan case
450g (1lb) grapes, black and green
*   (or 450g (1lb) fresh fruit tinned or*
*   bottled)*
575ml (1 pint) of custard (optional)

Glaze
½ pint juice from the fruit after
*   poaching*
OR
drained syrup from tin
OR
1 heaped tablespoon apricot jam
OR
sugar syrup

Facing page: Caramel Oranges (top), Blackberry Fluff (centre left) and Cherries in Wine (bottom).

second to warm the brandy through. Ignite, and let the flames die naturally. Serve at once. Serve hot with single cream.

Raspberry Jelly Mould

PREPARATION TIME: 8-10 minutes
plus setting

1 packet raspberry jelly
300ml (½ pint) milk
150ml (¼ pint) water
200g (8oz) fresh or thawed, frozen raspberries
150ml (¼ pint) water to melt jelly
Cream

Put the jelly into a saucepan with 150ml (¼ pint) water and melt slowly. Stand until the jelly is tepid, then slowly stir in 300ml (½ pint) of milk and 150ml (¼ pint) of water. Wet the jelly mould and fill with the fruit. Pour in the jelly and leave until set. To serve, decorate with any fruit, and cream.

Simple Trifles

PREPARATION TIME: 15 minutes

6 trifle sponges
3 tablespoons Cointreau or orange liqueur
3 oranges
4 tablespoons lemon curd
3 egg whites
6 lemon twists

Break trifle sponges into pieces and place in 6 individual dishes. Sprinkle each one with half a tablespoon of Cointreau. Peel the oranges. Chop them and remove all pith. Divide equally between the portions. Place the lemon curd in a bowl. Whisk the egg whites until stiff and fold them into the lemon curd. Spoon this mixture over each serving and decorate with twists of lemon. Chill and serve.

Halve and stone the grapes. Place them cut side down in alternate rings around a flan case. Glaze with one heaped tablespoon of warmed apricot jam, poured and brushed over the fruit. Alternatively, spread the base of the flan with 575ml (1 pint) of made custard before covering with fruit. Glaze with either apricot jam or sugar syrup.

Cherries in Wine

PREPARATION TIME: 5 minutes
COOKING TIME: 10 minutes

250g (1lb) cherries, stoned
½ teaspoon ground cinnamon
4 tablespoons sugar
300ml (½ pint) light red wine
4 tablespoons redcurrant jelly
2 teaspoons cornflour

Put the cherries, cinnamon, sugar and most of the wine into a heavy saucepan. Boil slowly. Mix the redcurrant jelly and cornflour with the rest of the wine and form into a paste before stirring into the saucepan. Simmer for three minutes, then remove from heat. Leave covered for five minutes. Serve cold.

Brandy Bananas

PREPARATION TIME: 10 minutes

75g (3oz) butter
3 tablespoons soft brown sugar
3 tablespoons lemon juice
6 bananas
3 tablespoons brandy
Single cream

Put the butter, sugar and lemon juice in a frying pan. Add the bananas and fry gently, making sure they are coated with the mixture. Add the brandy and cook for a

This page: Brandy Bananas (top left), Cherries Jubilee (centre right) and Spiced Pears (bottom).

Facing page: Simple Trifle (top left), Tarte Aux Fruits (top right), Redcurrant and Blackcurrant Compote (far right) and Raspberry Jelly Mould (bottom).

Stuffed Baked Peaches

PREPARATION TIME: 15 minutes

COOKING TIME: 30 minutes

OVEN: 180°C (350°F) Gas Mark 4

*6 large peaches, peeled, halved and
 stoned*
75g (3oz) macaroons, crushed
40g (1½oz) ground almonds
1 teaspoon finely grated orange rind
2 egg yolks
*40g (1½oz) butter, cut into small
 pieces*
225ml (7½ fl oz) sweet white wine

Put the peaches on a baking dish,
cut side up. In a small mixing bowl
put the macaroons, almonds,
orange rind and egg yolks. Mix
together and use to fill the peaches.
Put a knob of butter on top of each
peach. Pour the wine into the
baking dish and bake. Serve warm.

Fruit Salad with Cottage Cheese

PREPARATION TIME: 20 minutes

75g (3oz) cranberries
75g (3oz) raspberries
4 tablespoons orange juice
60g (2½oz) granulated sugar
2 tablespoons brandy
1 ogen melon
3 kiwi fruit
25g (1oz) icing sugar
200g (7oz) cottage cheese

Raspberry Sauce
200g (7oz) raspberries
75g (3oz) sugar
75ml (2½ fl oz) red wine
Small piece of lemon rind
Walnut pieces to decorate

Boil the cranberries, raspberries
and orange juice with the
granulated sugar for five minutes.
Strain the mixture through a sieve.
Stir in the brandy and cool. Peel
and slice the melon and kiwi fruit.
Arrange the fruit on individual
plates. Stir the icing sugar into the
cottage cheese and place a little on
top of each plateful of fruit. Chill.
Decorate using any of the fruit
contained in the sauce.

Raspberry Sauce
Purée the raspberries. Boil for 5
minutes adding the sugar and wine
and lemon rind. Continue to boil
for three minutes. Serve hot or
cold.

Baked Orange Rhubarb

PREPARATION TIME: 10 minutes

COOKING TIME: 45 minutes

OVEN: 160°C (325°F) Gas Mark 3

*1kg (2lb) rhubarb, cut into 2.5cm
 (1 inch) pieces*
*1 finely grated rind of, and juice of
 one orange*
6 tablespoons clear honey

Place the rhubarb in a baking dish
and sprinkle over the orange rind,
juice and honey. Cover and bake in
a moderate oven. Serve.

Plums Baked in Port

PREPARATION TIME: 5 minutes

COOKING TIME: 45 minutes

OVEN: 150°C (300°F) Gas Mark 2

1kg (2lb) plums, halved and stoned
100g (4oz) brown sugar
150ml (¼ pint) port

Place the plums in a baking dish.
Sprinkle over the sugar and port.
Cover them and bake in a cool
oven until the plums are tender.
Serve warm or lightly chilled.

Pêches Carmen

PREPARATION TIME: 10 minutes

8 ripe peaches
675g (1½lb) raspberries
2 tablespoons kirsch
75g (3oz) icing sugar

Slice the peaches into a serving
dish. Add the raspberries and
kirsch. Leave to stand for an hour
in a cool place. Spoon into
individual dishes and sprinkle with
icing sugar. Chill and serve with
cream.

Facing page: Highland Cream and Ginger Snaps (top), Stuffed Baked Peaches (centre) and Fruit Salad with Cottage Cheese (bottom).

This page: (left picture) Pèches Carmen (top), Stuffed Oranges (centre) and Plums in Port (bottom). (Right picture) Sour Cream Peaches (top), Ginger Roll (centre) and Baked Orange Rhubarb (bottom).

Sour Cream Peaches

PREPARATION TIME: 10 minutes

COOKING TIME: 10 minutes

6 large peaches, peeled, sliced and stoned
3 tablespoons brown sugar
½ teaspoon ground cinnamon
300ml (½ pint) sour cream
6 tablespoons granulated sugar

Divide the peach slices between 6 flameproof serving dishes. Mix together the brown sugar and cinnamon. Sprinkle this over the peaches. Spoon the sour cream over the top. Sprinkle a tablespoon of sugar over each portion. Grill quickly until the sugar melts and caramelises.

Ginger Roll

PREPARATION TIME: This dish should be started the night before required, to allow the ginger biscuits to absorb the rum.

36 ginger snap biscuits
6 tablespoons rum
600ml (1 pint) double cream
2 teaspoons ground ginger
2 teaspoons soft brown sugar
2 tablespoons ginger syrup (from stem ginger)
Stem ginger slices

Put the biscuits in a flat dish and sprinkle with rum. When the rum has been completely absorbed, whip the cream with the ground ginger and sugar and add the ginger syrup. Use some of the cream to sandwich together the biscuits.

Cover with the remaining cream and decorate with stem ginger slices. Serve.

Stuffed Oranges

PREPARATION TIME: 15 minutes

3 large oranges
2 dessert apples, peeled, cored and chopped
1½ tablespoons raisins
1½ tablespoons dates, chopped
1½ tablespoons nuts, toasted and chopped
1½ tablespoons soft brown sugar
180ml (6 fl oz) double cream
2 teaspoons icing sugar
Orange twists

Halve the oranges and scoop out the flesh, keeping the shells intact. Chop the flesh, discarding all the pith, and put it in a bowl. Add to the orange flesh the brown sugar, apple, raisins, dates and nuts. Mix well. Scoop the mixture back into the orange halves. Whip the cream with the icing sugar until it forms soft peaks. Spoon this cream on top of the orange mixture. Chill and serve. Decorate with twists of orange.

Highland Cream Served with Ginger Snaps

PREPARATION TIME: 15 minutes

4 tablespoons ginger marmalade
375ml (12 fl oz) double cream
4 tablespoons caster sugar
3 tablespoons whisky
3 tablespoons lemon juice
3 egg whites
Soft brown sugar
1 packet ginger snap biscuits

Divide the marmalade between serving dishes. Whip the cream, adding the caster sugar gradually. Fold in the whisky and lemon juice. Whisk the egg whites and fold into the cream. With a spoon, put a little of the cream mixture over the marmalade. Decorate with brown sugar and ginger snaps.

Orange Tart

PREPARATION TIME: 30 minutes
COOKING TIME: 25 minutes
OVEN: 190°C (375°F) Gas Mark 5

1 cooked pastry case
2 navel oranges, boiled
2 egg yolks, beaten
150g (6oz) sugar

To decorate
3 navel oranges
Apricot jam, melted

Purée the boiled oranges. Stir in the egg yolks and sugar. Slice the remaining three oranges. Fill the pastry case with the orange purée and decorate with slices of orange. Bake in a moderate oven until bubbling. Remove from oven and brush on melted apricot jam. Return to oven and bake for a further 10 minutes.

Fraises Escoffier

PREPARATION TIME: 15 minutes
plus chilling

1kg (2lb) strawberries
2 oranges
50g (2oz) sugar cubes
75ml (2½ fl oz) Grand Marnier

Hull and slice the strawberries; peel and slice the oranges. Mash half the strawberries with sugar cubes and Grand Marnier. Stir in the remaining fruit and chill for one hour. Serve in individual dishes.

Lemon Mousse

PREPARATION TIME: 6-10 minutes

150g (6oz) caster sugar
3 eggs, separated
5 lemons
12g (½oz) gelatine
2 tablespoons warm water

Put the grated rind of the lemons in a basin with the egg yolks and sugar. Beat until stiff. Beat the egg whites until they peak. Dissolve the gelatine in the water and mix with the egg yolk mixture. Beat until the mixture begins to set. Fold in the egg whites. Fill the glasses with mousse. Serve chilled.

Fraises Escoffier (right),
Orange Tart (centre right)
and Lemon Mousse (far
right).

EXTRA INFORMATION

Strawberry Sauce

50g (2oz) sugar
1½ tablespoons lemon juice
1½ tablespoons brandy
250g (9oz) strawberries

Place sugar, lemon juice and brandy in a pan. Place over a low heat until sugar dissolves. Sieve strawberries to remove seeds and combine with syrup. Cool.

Caramel Chips

50g (2oz) caster sugar

Put the sugar in a heavy saucepan and heat gently until the sugar liquifies and turns golden. Pour quickly onto foil and leave until cold. Break the chips with a rolling pin and use for decoration.

Apricot Purée

3 tablespoons sugar
1 tablespoon water
1 teaspoon lime juice
2 tablespoons apricot brandy
250g (9oz) well-ripened apricots

Combine sugar, water, lime juice and apricot brandy in pan. Dissolve sugar over low heat. Cool. Sieve or purée apricots in blender. Combine with syrup.

Chocolate Sauce

100g (4oz) plain dark chocolate
2 tablespoons milk
2 rounded tablespoons golden
  syrup

Melt the chocolate in a bowl over a pan of simmering water. Beat in the milk and golden syrup until glossy.

Sugar Syrup *(medium syrup)*

75g (3oz) sugar (granulated)
150ml (5 fl oz) water

Boiling sugar for dessert making can be easily done without a thermometer. Mix together water and sugar in a small saucepan and boil until the mixture begins to thicken.

Index